LET'S AGREE TO DISAGREE

A REVIEW OF ISSUES WE WILL NEVER AGREE ON, BUT LET'S MOVE ON

BRADLEY W. RASCH

ISBN: 1977508324

ISBN 13: 9781977508324

CONTENTS

INTRODUCTION

———

God knows there is a lot we disagree about. There are cable channels, and even that rare endangered species, the AM radio talk show "personality", that exist to amplify, nurture, and encourage those disagreements. It's as though we have forgotten that we have anything in common with others, and it almost seems as though we have lost sight of the belief that we are all in this together.

Now, especially if you are a member of Congress, you can be voted out of office for agreeing with or even listening to an opponent on " the other side of the aisle". Heavens to Betsy, how did we get to this point? Will we ever again respect people that listen? Will we ever again see virtue in " agreeing to disagree", a prerequisite for getting things done? Will compromise always be seen as a weakness, and not strength? Is it better to move forward, or just stand on your principles, and never progress?

This book will explore twenty-six areas of disagreement, one for each letter of the alphabet, that we may never reach a consensus on. Hopefully, after reading this book, the reader may find value in agreeing to disagree and moving on, and see that course of action as strength, and not a weakness.

This book has three target audiences:

1. The follower of current events with strong beliefs, that would like to " move on", and work towards agreeing to disagree so that can be accomplished.
2. The college student that wants to really explore critical thinking, and maybe impress the heck out of their professor on an essay test.
3. The casual reader that loves to be challenged and seek out information to challenge others.

I

ABORTION

———

It is not possible to begin our discussion with a more controversial, emotional, or divisive topic than abortion. Good people on all sides of this issue have extraordinarily strong views on this topic, and people that ordinarily listen to divergent viewpoints, often will not do so on when discussing this subject.

Politicians have been elected or voted out of office due to their views; much fund raising (especially by the political class) has occurred regarding this procedure, and many presidential candidates have cited this issue, and this issue alone, as something they would consider when appointing a Supreme Court Justice.

From a moral viewpoint abortion often involves a discussion of when life begins. At conception? At the age of viability (when a fetus can survive outside of the womb), or, as in the view of Jewish mothers, when the child graduates from medical school?

Abortion was widely practiced in this country before the 1880's. By this time most US states banned or restricted the procedure. Doctors that did not want competition from midwifes supported these restrictions. Abortion also became an issue because many wanted more white Northern European babies in our society.

Economics then and now are an important determiner of access to safe abortion services. In times of great abortion restrictions at home, the wealthy often traveled to modern first world countries for abortion services, often while campaigning for domestic restrictions.

Before 1973 and Roe v Wade, many medical professionals risked jail time, loss of license, and fines to provide safe services to those who could not afford to travel to other countries for abortions.

In the late 1960's, Clergy Consultation Services on Abortion was established to refer women to safe abortions, because so many were dying from unsafe procedures.

From 1967 to 1973 states began making abortions more difficult to obtain. In 1976 the Hyde Amendment codified and prohibited federal money from being utilized to provide abortion services. This had a significant impact on; you guessed it, low-income people.

From 2010 to 2015 many states enacted TRAP (Targeted Regulation of Abortion Providers) laws. These laws regulated the size of hallways, and hundreds of other things, in abortion provider facilities, in an effort to end a supreme court granted right, through attrition.

Regardless of one's moral stance on abortion, it must be recognized that the wealthy will always have access to abortion, and the poor will have limited access when restrictions occur. The poor will then seek unsafe abortions, which will lead to increased maternal deaths. A point to consider for the pro-life point of view.

Those that refer to themselves as pro-life would be much more persuasive if, as part of their advocacy, they pushed for accessible and affordable daycare, nutrition, housing, and medical care for infants. In other words, if they were not just friends of the fetus, but also advocates for the birthed child.

Those that call themselves pro-choice may be more persuasive if they did not suggest that the anti-abortion lobby were simple people trying to push their moral beliefs on others.

There are certainly reasonable and good people on all sides of this issue. Just as certainly, there is demagogy, manipulators, opportunists and hypocrites on both sides.

Discussion of this issue by decision makers and lawmakers would be better served when more women are on the panels.

Perhaps this is an area where we can agree to disagree, so progress in other areas can be made. Total agreement by all people is unlikely to ever occur.

2

BUSINESS

———

On January 17, 1925 Calvin Coolidge (" Silent Cal") famously said, " The Business of America is Business." Right? Well. Close. Silent Cal was, in reality, misquoted. What he really said was "The chief business of the American people is business".

We are, in fact, a nation of business, capitalism, and as Gordon Gekko would say " Greed is good" or many of us think it is. Actually, to be technically correct, Michael Douglas actually said greed is good when portraying the fictional Gordon Gekko.

Two areas of contention in business may never be settled. CEO (and management) pay vs. worker pay, and long-term strategy vs. short-term strategy. Let us explore these two areas of contention.

Corporations are under great pressure, and are arguably really required; to put their shareholders needs first. Period.

A CEO, a corporate board, will not be serving long if they do not look out for their stockholders'. How do you look out for your stockholders? Give them cash, the sooner the better. Even if you have to borrow it.

A company that may be well served by making massive investments in research and development, or even pollution control technology to put themselves in a better position in their industry ten or twenty years down the road will be under pressure to not spend that money so that they can reward shareholders in the present with dividends, and their CEO's with significant bonuses. The shareholders, many of them at least, will be all in on short-term thinking that puts money in their pockets now. Certainly a large bonus today for a corporate officer will be welcome over an investment that will not payoff for the company in a generation. This short-term approach is good for many in the present but not good for our nations future well being especially when we are competing with nations willing and able to think long-term.

Psychologists have made an important discovery. The marshmallow test. Give a very young child the option of one marshmallow now, or several if they wait a few minutes. The toddlers' that choose to wait to earn more marshmallows, those that can delay their need for gratification, by all measures five years, ten years, twenty or thirty years down the line do better in life. It looks as though American business may have failed the marshmallow test.

Another area of controversy, ostensibly unsolvable, is CEO pay. Many feel it is un-American to even talk about limiting it. Don't even think about it, you communist! Others think maybe it has gotten a little out of hand.

In 1965, the typical CEO made 20 times what the average worker made. Now he or she makes 510.7 times what the average worker makes.

If we were back in the mind set of the 1960's many workers would be making livable wages. But is it fair to restrict a CEO to a 20 million dollar annual salary when they could be making 40 million?

In 2016 the top three CEO's by salary made 98 million dollars, 68.6 million, and 41 million dollars per year. This did not include many other perks. Number three on the list was the CEO of Disney. We can assume there were a lot of " Hi Ho's, Hi Ho's sung on the way to work. Number ten on the list made a paltry 28.2 million dollars a year.

If we reverted to the ratios of the 1960's many workers could live a better lifestyle, and the CEO's would still be making a good coin.

The long-term vs. short-term debate and the issue of CEO pay is most probably not solvable, much to our detriment. Perhaps we should agree to disagree and sing Hi Ho Hi Ho on the way to our minimum wage jobs anyhow.

3

CANNABIS

Before we begin our discussion of weed I must bring up one fact: George Washington, the father of our country, grew hemp on his farm. He also grew tobacco and was a rather prominent whisky distiller. (He did not have a wooden tooth, that is a myth. He did have many pairs of false teeth made of other materials, but that is neither here nor there.) That said, the question is this: should cannabis use be legal or illegal?

Concerns about cannabis include that it may be a "gateway" to the abuse of other drugs, loss of ambition, brain damage, impaired driving, schizophrenia, and a host of other potential issues.

Supporters of marijuana legalization point to the use of a cannabis as a pain killer, a nausea reducer for patients receiving chemotherapy, an effective treatment for some that suffer from PTSD, a means of helping people with epilepsy, treatment of stroke victims and to the use of a product to help you unwind and relax that may be safer and less addicting than a couple of daily glasses of wine.

Here are some facts to consider:

1. Since marijuana has been criminalized (its use in some states is now legal *at the state level*) there has been very little research as to its efficacy and uses to treat a variety of disorders. This prohibition of research has often been due to federal regulation, and was decided upon for political, not scientific reasons.
2. A tremendous number of people have been incarcerated for marijuana use that harmed no one, and they have broken no other laws. Their potential to contribute to their families and society is limited, and it has cost the country billions to prosecute and jail them.
3. Wealthy people can often avoid the legal consequences of being collared for weed possession, poor people often cannot.

4. Preliminary research shows that weed use may be less addicting than alcohol use, that there is less impaired driving with marijuana than with alcohol, and that an over dose of weed may not be possible, or at least less possible than with overuse of alcohol.
5. Early research suggests that it may not be a good idea for teens to use weed, because it impacts their brain development. Certainly, alcohol use has a similar reason for caution.
6. Wine is used in many religious rituals. So is marijuana
    (By Native Americans and others-no not college freshman).

The bottom line is that we do not yet know of all of the potential medical benefits of marijuana, because there is a paucity of legitimate scientific studies. We do know that it is quite beneficial in some cases for some maladies. We know that people can abuse weed. They can also abuse alcohol and prescription drugs.

Hopefully we can at least support good quality scientific research on the medicinal use of cannabis. Especially for conditions that are lacking effective treatment options.

As to recreational use, and allowing it as an alternative to wine, beer, whiskey, and hard lemonade? Let's agree to disagree.

Do we lock up the small time user that has harmed no one and has committed no other crime? It seems we may have to agree to disagree on this as well.

One final note: we have had at least two Presidents and two Supreme Court Justices that have used cannabis. We have had several more Presidents that have overindulged in alcohol in a sometimes-worrisome manner.

4

DEATH PENALTY

—

The debate about the death penalty has been long, vigorous, and important. It will probably never end. (The debate, that is).

The most recent respected statistics on the death penalty go back to 2016, a year in which 1,032 people were executed worldwide. Here is a rank ordering of nations, the top five, in terms of state sponsored executions:

1. China
2. Iran
3. Saudi Arabia
4. Iraq
5. Pakistan

Notice the United States is not in the top five. The USA was in seventh place that year, the first time the USA had not been in the top five since 2006.

It should be noted that 141 countries have, effectively, abolished the death penalty.

In 2016 worldwide, 3117 death sentences were handed down.

The worldwide statistics above should be treated with caution, as the statistics from China are somewhat suspect.

There are many arguments in favor of the death penalty:

1. It is an effective deterrent. Studies show that this is true. However, it is an expensive alternative. Execution actually costs significantly more than the death penalty (legal fees and the like).

2. Religion supports the death penalty (the eye for an eye argument) Yes, the Bible speaks to an eye for an eye, but it also speaks to forgiveness and turning the other cheek.
3. Families deserve closure. Indeed they do. Are there other ways we can explore to help them in this regard?
4. The killer deserves to die. Many would certainly agree here. But certainly not all, for reasons discussed below.

There are also arguments against the death penalty:

1. Life without parole may be an even harsher punishment and a less expensive one.
2. Poor quality legal defense is provided to many poor defendants. Innocent people have been convicted and executed.
3. The death penalty is applied randomly. In an election year a liberal Governor may want to appear strong and move towards the middle of the political spectrum and executions may increase. A conservative Governor may want to appeal to the base, and state sponsored killing increases.
4. The mentally ill are often executed. Are they responsible for their actions? This is certainly another debate in a sense.
5. The state executes people in our name. Is this okay with everyone?

The death penalty is controversial, especially so in election years. There are points to consider:

1. Are there better ways to help the loved ones of the murdered to achieve closure?
2. As a society are we okay with the state killing in our name.
3. Is it acceptable that some innocent people will be executed in our name?
4. Are we comfortable with poor defendants and minorities being more likely to being executed due to a lack of access to high quality legal defense?
5. Can we recognize that it is a political issue as well as a moral issue, and still accept it?

Much political fund raising occurs due to the emotions pro or con the death penalty stokes. How comfortable are we with this?

This life or death issue seems also to be an area where we may have to agree to disagree. As with many issues of this type, it is likely we will just decide that it is a " local Issue".

5

ELECTORAL COLLEGE

—

The Electoral College is a quirky American institution that's been with us since the beginning of the republic. Sometimes it causes controversy, at other times it is totally unnoticed.

When a state certifies a winner of its overall popular vote, Our Electoral College meets and fulfills its obligations a month or so after the election and few notice or pay heed. On occasion, though, we do notice and do pay heed – a great deal.

How does our Electoral College work?

Our Constitution does *not* mandate the election of the American president by popular vote. It provides for popular election of *presidential electors*. Each candidate who qualifies for any state's ballot must designate certain people who will serve as his or her electors if that candidate wins the popular vote in that specific state.

That winner is entitled to send all his or her electors to that state's capital, where they will officially record their votes for their candidate. All the electors in all the states do it on the same day by law, the first Monday after the second Wednesday of December.

In these meetings in each state, the winner of the statewide popular vote usually takes all the Electoral College votes, a rule stretching back to the year 1824.

Two states, Nebraska and Maine, have used a different system, giving two electoral votes to the statewide winner and one to the winner of each of the state's congressional districts. This is allowed as the Constitution makes provisions for individual states to determine the manner of their elections. Other states have recently explored doing this as well.

Maine is comprised of two Congressional Districts, therefore, its vote can be split 3-1. Nebraska has three districts, so it could split 4-1 or 3-2. Nebraska had a 4-1 split in 2008, when its Omaha-metro district voted for Mr. Obama while the other districts went for Mr. McCain.

Some states have also considered a very unique idea: Casting the state's electoral votes for the candidate that wins the national popular vote. This would serve to undercut the Electoral College's "indirect democracy" and support the idea of a *national* choice, regardless of state lines.

Currently, here is how our Electoral College votes are apportioned to the states: Each state is assigned a number equal to its Senate seats (always two) plus its seats in the House of Representatives.

That means the seven states with only enough population to qualify for one House seat will get three votes each in the Electoral College. Arguably, an over representation. So much for the concept of " one man one vote". California, with 53 seats in the House, gets 55 electoral votes, and Texas' 36 seats mean it gets 38 electoral votes.

This is the reason why, after the U.S. expanded to include 50 states, the Electoral College had 535 seats, the same as the total of members of Congress (Senate and House). It now has 538, because in 1961 the 23rd Amendment to the Constitution added three for the District of Columbia, which had previously been without a voice in choosing the president of the United States (and which is still without a vote in either the Senate or the House). Ironic that our nations capitol was disenfranchised for so long.

If the Electoral College seems antiquated or unfair, you are not alone and are certainly in agreement with supporters of Al Gore and Hillary Clinton

Many have thought from the very beginning that the Electoral College is an undemocratic concept that the people could not or should not be trusted to vote directly for a national leader.

Rational as the "indirect method" may have been at one time, at the beginning of our republic, it has come to be viewed as anachronistic in the extreme. Were anyone to propose that we start electing other office holders, for example, governors, by a similar method they would be disrespected in the extreme.

In 2016 Hillary Clinton had 65, 853, 516 popular votes and Donald Trump had 62, 984, 825 votes. Trump, however, won the Electoral College, so he became president. This has happened four other times. In 2000 when Al Gore got 48.4% of the popular vote to 47.9% for George W. Bush (a margin of about 500,000 votes). After a struggle over the count in one state (Florida) that went all the way to the Supreme Court, Bush was declared the winner with 271 votes in the Electoral College – one more than the minimum for a majority. In reality then, Bush became president because he carried the Supreme Court, but that is certainly another issue.

Our system of 50 separate state elections encourages candidates to concentrate their campaign time and resources on a handful of " battleground states". These are generally medium-to-large states where neither party has an overwhelming advantage. That means some large Electoral vote heavy states (California, Texas, New York, Illinois) are largely neglected, while a few others (Florida, Pennsylvania, Ohio and North Carolina) see more of the candidates and their high level supporters than the rest of the country combined. Small states are often left off the campaign trail. This, despite the fact that each citizen's vote is supposed to be worth as much as any other's.

What if there is a tie in the Electoral College, which is infinitely more probable than a tie in the popular vote? Our system can produce a tie (269-269). This has not happened yet but such an outcome is a distinct possibility.

What would happen then? It would mean no candidate had a majority, a prospect that could also happen if a third party candidate won at least one state, depriving either of the major party candidates of a majority. This came relatively close to happening in the1968 election.

An Electoral College that failed to produce a majority winner would trigger a constitutional provision by which our president would be chosen by the House of Representatives. This would be entertaining to observe. That vote would be taken when the newly elected Congress convenes in January, and it would be a vote of the 50 state delegations *with each state having one vote.* That's correct the Wyoming delegation (one member) would have the same say as the 38-member Texas contingent or the 53 members from California.

This, too, strikes many as unfair, not to mention flagrantly undemocratic. Again, so much for the concept of one man one vote.

Suffice it to say that the Constitution, as written way back in 1787 and amended often since that time, respects the rights of states as entities unto themselves. Perhaps the framers did not envision population disparities between the states reaching to 100 to 1 and beyond.

They certainly understood at the time that New York and Virginia were far more populous than Delaware and Rhode Island. And they clearly respected the rights of all the former colonies to maintain their identities, a philosophy that may have made more sense then than now. . This led to the "Great Compromise" by which all states got two seats in the Senate and the House was apportioned according to population. That deal, fashioned by Sherman and Ellsworth, two delegates from Connecticut, was credited with getting the Constitution completed and ratified.

There is an additional issue about the Electoral College to consider. It is the notion of the "faithless elector," the person who pledges to vote for a certain candidate but comes to the state Capitol and votes for someone else – a different candidate or a person who was not even on the ballot. This is possible and has happened.

Fortunately, Such anomalies do not happen often. It happened once recently in 1988, when an elector pledged to Democrat Michael Dukakis voted instead for his running mate, Lloyd Bentsen. It was a rather meaningless gesture that did not matter to the outcome, except to demand an asterisk and an explanation. But what if several others Electors decided to be " faithless?"

In a very close election, such as the election of 2000, a faithless elector or two might be enough to change the outcome – or at least to send the contest into the House.

As it was, the official tally that year was only 537 because one elector did not vote at all. It did not change the outcome, but it showed how easily the system is subject to breakdown.

We have had a number of elections where the person that won the most popular votes lost the election because they lost the Electoral College:

- 1824: Andrew Jackson, the popular vote winning Democratic candidate lost out to John Quincy Adams.
- 1876: Democratic candidate Samuel Tilden, despite winning the popular votes was narrowly defeated in Electoral College by Republican Rutherford Hayes.

- 1886: Democrat Grover Cleveland, winner of popular vote, lost out to Benjamin Harrison in terms of electoral college votes.
- 2000: Democrat Al Gore lost to Republican George Bush.
- 2016: Clinton lost to Trump, despite winning the popular vote by a considerable margin.

Here are some arguments in favor of the Electoral College:

1. In the long term your power, as an individual voter is greater in a divided election than in a direct election.

With 50 states and over 100 million voters, figuring out how citizens share power in an election is a huge undertaking. To make it easier, lets invent an imaginary nation of Mudcat, a fictional country we just made up.

Mudcat is divided into three

States: North, Central and South. Each state has one million voters. The nation has two major political parties: the Apples and the Oranges.

How much of a voice do you have in a nation-wide election? It depends on whether the election is *direct* or *divided*.

In a direct election, it's easy to calculate the power of your voice. You have one vote. There are three million total voters. Thus, your influence is **1 in 3,000,000.**

In a divided election, it's a little bit more difficult. Your vote helps your candidate carry your state. But in order for a candidate to win, they need to carry two of the three states. You need another state to join you.

Let's say you live in Central Mudcat, and you support the Apple candidate. Your influence in your home state is 1 in 1,000,000—there are 1,000,000 voters, and you are one of them. If the Apple candidate carries a second state, your influence there is 0 in 1,000,000—that state also has 1 million voters, but you aren't one of them. So, your influence in the two states Apple needs to win is **1 in 2,000,000**.

In other words, **your vote is 50% more powerful in the divided election than in a direct election**. Each vote cast in this system has the same power as 1.5 votes in the direct system.

And, strangely enough, the same holds true for every voter in the country. The divided system has made the entire citizenry 1.5 times more powerful.

How can it be that everyone gets stronger and no one gets weaker? It has to do with the minimum number of votes a candidate needs to win.

- In a direct election, the candidate needs one more than half of the total votes cast—in this case, that's 1,500,001.
- In a divided election, they need one more than half of the votes *in only part of the nation*. In our example, that's 500,001 in each of two states, or 1,000,002 total—a smaller number.

In each case, you as a citizen get one vote. Your vote moves your candidate one step closer to victory. But in a divided election that journey, though more complicated, ultimately takes a lot fewer steps. Fewer votes are needed to win, so each vote takes on more importance.

The Electoral College creates a clear winner in cases where the popular vote is very close.

On November 8, 1960, America went to the polls to elect a new president. John F. Kennedy beat Richard M. Nixon in one of the closest elections in US history. More than 68 million citizens cast their votes, and Kennedy came out ahead by less than 2/10ths of 1%. There were widespread allegations of vote stealing on both sides, and many calls for a recount.

If this had been a direct election, a national recount of 68 million votes would have taken months, and opened up more potential for fraud. But because the Electoral College divided one big national election into 50 individual state elections, recounts were only pursued in a few states where the vote was closest. And because Kennedy had a huge lead in Electoral votes—318 to 219—Nixon would have had to win just about all the challenges to change the outcome of the election. It soon became clear that wouldn't happen, and most of the recounts were dropped. The Electoral College took what had been a virtual tie in the popular vote and turned it into a clear victory for Kennedy.

Six times in American history, the top vote getter for president beat the challenger by less than 1%. If we had a national direct election, verifying these results would have required a national recount. Under the Electoral College, there would only be recounts in a couple of close states, or perhaps no recounts at all.

In fact, the Electoral College almost always produces a wider margin of victory that the popular vote totals. This makes the election seem more clear-cut, giving the president the mandate needed to lead the country.

In most cases, the Electoral College forces candidates to win not just a majority, but also a super-majority. They can't just win a majority of individual votes; they have to win a majority of votes in a majority of states (or, at least, a majority of large states). This helps legitimize the election.

The Electoral College forces candidates to pay attention to all voters. They can't just focus on a few big cities. They have to win entire states, and lots of them.

In every election, a few states are too close to call. These are known as "swing states," and candidates pay a great deal of attention to them. Which states will swing changes every four years? Over time, pretty much every state has its moment in the spotlight. (In a direct election, candidates would always focus on large population centers, and those don't change nearly as rapidly.)

The Electoral College protects and empowers minorities. Candidates might ignore a small minority in a national election. But groups concentrated in specific areas can have a significant influence in those states. By forcing candidates to compete for states rather than for individual votes, the Electoral College system gives minorities a stronger voice.

But perhaps the most far-reaching consequence of the Electoral College is that it has led to the development of two political parties that strive for broad appeal. Most other democracies have dozens of parties, many with very narrow agendas. With so many parties dividing the legislature, it can be difficult to get them to agree on anything. But the Electoral College requires a candidate to win a majority of electoral votes. If there were three or more parties that would almost never happen. Thus, American politics evolved to have two national parties, each of which needs to appeal to as many people as possible.

There is also argument against the Electoral College:

- The possibility of electing a minority president
- The risk of so-called "faithless" Electors,

- The possible role of the Electoral College in depressing voter turn-out, and
- Its failure to accurately reflect the national popular will.

We are hesitant as a people to change such fundamental structures of our democracy. Many are afraid that opening up things to change may bring about change for the worse. Others believe that the founding fathers were divinely inspired, thus, it is sacrilegious to

Change something so fundamental.

Why do we have the Electoral College in the first place?

The Electoral College was created for two reasons. Reasons that were deemed important a long time ago at the founding of our nation. The first purpose of the Electoral College was to create a buffer between population and the selection of a President. The second as part of the structure of the government that gave extra power to the smaller states, an issue that was extremely relevant in the early days of our republic.

The first reason that the founders created the Electoral College is very difficult to understand in present day America. The founding fathers were afraid of direct election to the Presidency. They feared a tyrant could manipulate public opinion and come to power. Hamilton wrote in the Federalist Papers:

It was equally desirable, that the immediate election should be made by men most capable of analyzing the qualities adapted to the station, and acting under circumstances favorable to deliberation, and to a judicious combination of all the reasons and inducements which were proper to govern their

choice. A small number of persons, selected by their fellow-citizens from the general mass, will be most likely to possess the information and discernment requisite to such complicated investigations. It was also peculiarly desirable to afford as little opportunity as possible to tumult and disorder. This evil was not least to be dreaded in the election of a magistrate, who was to have so important an agency in the administration of the government as the President of the United States. But the precautions, which have been, so happily concerted in the system under consideration, promise an effectual security against this mischief.

Hamilton and the other founders believed that the electors would be able to insure that only a qualified person becomes President. They believed that with the Electoral College no one would be able to manipulate the citizenry. In other words, they did not trust the common man. It would act as check on an electorate that might be duped. Hamilton and the other founders did not trust the population to make the right choice. The founders also were of the belief that the Electoral College had the advantage of being a group that met only once and thus could not be manipulated over time by foreign governments or others.

The Electoral College is also part of compromises made at the convention to satisfy the small states. This rationale cannot be overstated. It was very relevant then, not so much now. Under the system of the Electoral College each state had the same number of electoral votes as they have representative in Congress, thus no state could have less then 3.

The result of this system is that in one election the state of Wyoming cast about 210,000 votes, and thus each elector represented 70,000 votes, while in California approximately 9,700,000 votes were cast for 54 votes, thus representing 179,000 votes per electorate. Obviously this creates an unfair advantage to voters in the small states whose votes actually count more then those people living in medium and large states.

One aspect of the electoral system that is not mandated in the constitution is the fact that the winner takes all the votes in the state. Therefore, it makes no difference if you win a state by 50.1% or by 80% of the vote you receive the same number of electoral votes. This can be a recipe for one individual to win some states by large pluralities and lose others by small number of votes, and thus this is an easy scenario for one candidate winning the popular vote while another winning the electoral vote. This winner take all methods used in picking electors has been decided by the states themselves. This trend took place over the course of the 19th century.

While there are obvious problems with the Electoral College and there are some advantages to it, changing it is very unlikely. It would take a constitutional amendment ratified by 3/4 of states to change the system. As we know, legislators today cannot even agree on what to have for lunch. It is hard to imagine the smaller states agreeing. One-way of modifying the system s to eliminate the winner takes all part of it. The method that the states vote for the Electoral College is not mandated by the constitution but is decided by the states.

Two states currently do not use the winner take all system, Maine and Nebraska. It would be difficult but not totally impossible to get other states to change their systems, unfortunately the party that has the advantage in the state is unlikely to agree to a unilateral change.

For the reasons discussed above, it appears as though the Electoral College, and the debate about it, is here to stay. It seems we will have to agree to disagree on its appropriateness. A few things are for certain: It is hard to explain to foreigners that the beacon of democracy allows someone with less votes than their opponents to win an election, and that we are unlikely to change this system when smaller states or a political party may benefit from its continuation.

6

FOREIGN AID

—

Another issue that comes up very election cycle is the issue of foreign aid. Should we do it? Does charity begin at home? What is in it for us? Isn't it just the right thing to do? Can we afford it? Can we afford not to do it?

What exactly is foreign aid? Foreign aid is simply anything we give to another country, or any action we take that may help another country. Solicited or unsolicited. Is there a quid pro quo? Usually YES.

Foreign aid is not just money. It can be food delivery, infrastructure development, disaster relief, healthcare training, agricultural research assistance, and many other things. Helping a nation build a dam, or consulting with them about doing so. Providing technical support. Foreign aid takes many forms.

Foreign aid often involves helping a nation cope with the aftermath of a disaster. This aid may even flow to wealthy nations in their time of need. About 2/3 of foreign aid flows through our State Department and agencies like USAID. About 35 percent is funneled thru the Department of Defense to bolster the military of another nation, assist in anti-narcotic actions, deal with an insurgency (that may eventually threaten us) and other such activities.

What is the breakdown on what our foreign aid is used for?

Political 11 percent
This aid is used to promote democracy (hopefully not to encourage the use of an Electoral College).
To facilitate peace talks.
To support human rights organizations.
Similar uses.

Security 35 percent.
Strengthen the military of the recipient nation. (We have learned the dangers to us of a failed state).
Anti-narcotic missions.
Anti-terror missions.

General Development 35 percent.
Infrastructure development.
Helping the recipient nation to deal with its long-term needs.

Humanitarian 16 percent.
Food, shelter, etc. for immediate disaster relief.

The Pros of foreign aid:
It alleviates poverty.
It promotes friendship.
It helps people in crisis.
It helps other nations become more independent.
It can help stop the spread of disease that can find its way here.

The Cons of foreign aid:
Loans can put a nation in debt to us, and they may resent us for that, even if the terms of the loan were generous.
Many Americans feel it does no good. The receiving nation is not improving; they are still poor, and they
do not seem overly grateful.
Nations we do not help may become bitter.
Corrupt individuals, even the recipient nations government, siphon much of the aid off.

In a highly interdependent world, we have much to gain from other nations being strong economically, and free. We are so interconnected that a disease outbreak on the other side of the world will soon threaten us. Historically, large aid projects have benefited us; the Marshall plan after World War II is an excellent example. The aid we delivered led to countries strong enough to trade with us. This benefited our industries that could export. These stronger nations became valuable allies and friends.

Foreign aid will always be a political football.
Yet another area where we will have to agree to disagree.

7

GUN CONTROL

After abortion, there may be no topic more controversial or divisive in our country than gun control. No discussion of gun control can occur without considering the second amendment, text sacred to many Americans.

The second amendment states:

"A well regulated Militia, being necessary to the security of a free State, the right of the people to keep and bear Arms, shall not be infringed."

Pro gun control points:

THE SECOND AMMENDMENT TO THE CONSTITUTION DOES *NOT* GIVE AN ABSOLUTE RIGHT FOR ANY PERSON TO BEAR ARMS. Gun control laws, or, perhaps more appropriately gun regulation laws, are as old or older than the Second Amendment. Examples of gun control at the time of colonial America included criminalizing the transfer of guns to Catholics, slaves, indentured servants, and Native Americans; regulations about the storage of gun powder in Private homes; banning loaded guns in homes in Boston and mandating participation in the formal gathering of troops and door-to-door surveys about guns owned. In the June 26, 2008 *District of Columbia et al. v. Heller* US Supreme Court majority opinion, Justice Antonin Scalia, LLB, wrote, "Like most rights, the right secured by the Second Amendment is not unlimited. From Blackstone through the 19th-century cases, pundits and courts often explained that the right was not a right to keep and carry any weapon whatsoever in any manner whatsoever and for whatever purpose... nothing in our opinion should be taken to cast doubt on longstanding prohibitions on the possession of firearms by felons and the mentally ill, or laws forbidding the carrying of firearms in sensitive places such as schools and government buildings, or laws imposing conditions and qualifications on the commercial sale of arms."]On June 9, 2016 the US Ninth Circuit Court of Appeals ruled 7-4 that "the right of the general public to carry a concealed firearm in public is not, and never has been, protected by the Second Amendment," thus upholding a law requiring a permitting process and "good cause" for concealed carry licenses in the state of California.

GUN CONTOL LAWS WILL REDUCE GUN RELATED DEATHS. There were 464,033 total gun deaths between 1999 and 2013: 270,237 suicides (58.2% of total deaths); 174,773 homicides (37.7%); and 9,983 accidental deaths (2.2%). Guns were the leading cause of death by homicide (66.6% of all homicides) and by suicide (52.2% of all suicides). Firearms were the 12th leading cause of all deaths, representing 1.3% of total deaths topping liver disease, hypertension, and Parkinson's disease, as well as deaths from fires, drowning, and machinery accidents. David Frum, *Daily Beast* and CNN contributor, stated, "American children under age 15 were nine times more likely to die of a gun accident than children in other advanced wealthy countries… About 200 Americans go to emergency rooms every day with gunshot wounds." A study published in the *American Journal of Public Health* found that "legal purchase of a handgun appears to be associated with a long-lasting increased risk of violent death" a March 10, 2016 *Lancet* study, implementing federal universal background checks could reduce firearm deaths by a projected 56.9%; background checks for ammunition purchases could reduce deaths by a projected 80.7%; and gun identification requirements could reduce deaths by a projected 82.5%.

IF HIGH CAPACITY MAGAZINES ARE PROHIBITED OR REGULATED, MASS MURDERS CAN BE AVOIDED. A *Mother Jones* investigation found that high-capacity magazines were used in at least 50% of the 62 mass shootings between 1982 and 2012. When high-capacity magazines were used in mass shootings, the death rate rose 63% and the injury rate rose 156%. David H. Chipman, Senior Vice President of Public Safety for ShotSpotter and former Bureau of Alcohol, Tobacco, Firearms, and Explosives (ATF) agent, stated that a high-capacity magazine "turns a killer into a killing machine." Some gang members use high-capacity magazines, such as 30 rounds or even 90 rounds, to compensate for lack of accuracy and maximize the chance to harm. Often criminals can "out gun" our police.

GUN CONTROL LAWS CAN PROTECT WOMEN FROM ABUSE. Five women are murdered with guns every day in the United States. A woman's risk of being murdered increases 500% if a gun is present during a domestic dispute. During the Iraq and Afghanistan wars, 5,364 US soldiers were killed in action between Oct. 7, 2001 and Jan. 28, 2015; between 2001 and 2012 6,410 women were killed with a gun by an intimate partner in the United States. A study in 2003 of 23 populous high-income countries found that 86% of women killed by firearms were in the United States and American women are 11.4 times more likely to be the victims of gun homicides 57% of mass shootings involved domestic violence. For example, the 2011 mass shooting at a Seal Beach, CA hair salon reportedly began because of the shooter's custody battle with his ex-wife who was a hair stylist at the salon. Thirty-one states do not ban convicted misdemeanor stalkers from owning guns and 41 states do not force convicted domestic abusers from giving up guns they already own. 76% of women murdered and 85% of women who survived a murder attempt by an intimate partner were stalked in the year before the murder or murder attempt.

GUNS ARE USED FOR SELF-DEFENSE VERY RARELY. Of the 29,618,300 violent crimes committed between 2007 and 2011, 0.79% of victims (235,700) protected themselves with a threat of use or use of a firearm, the least-employed protective behavior. In 2010 there were 230 "justifiable homicides" in which a private citizen used a firearm to kill a felon, compared to 8,275 criminal gun homicides (or, 36 criminal homicides for every "justifiable homicide"). Of the 84,495,500 property crimes committed between 2007 and 2011, 0.12% of victims (103,000) protected themselves with a threat of use or use of a firearm.

LEGAL FOREARMS ARE OFTEN STOLEN AND USED BY CRIMINALS. A June 2013 Institute of Medicine (IOM) report states "almost all guns used in criminal acts enter circulation via initial legal transaction." Between 2005 and 2010, 1,400,000 guns were stolen from American homes during property crimes (including burglary and car theft), a yearly average of 232,400. Ian Ayres, JD, PhD, and John J. Donohue, JD, PhD,

Professors of Law at Yale Law School and Stanford Law School respectively, state, "with guns being a product that can be easily carried away and quickly sold at a relatively high fraction of the initial cost, the presence of more guns can actually serve as a stimulus to burglary and theft. Even if the gun owner had a permit to carry a concealed weapon and would never use it in furtherance of a crime, is it likely that the same can be said for the burglar who steals the gun?"

GUN CONTROL LAWS CAN REDUCE THE COSTS OF GUN VIOLENCE. According to the Pacific Institute for Research and Evaluation (PIRE), in 2010, gun violence cost each person in the United States roughly $564 and the US government $5.5 billion in lost tax revenue; $4.7 billion in court costs; $1.4 billion in Medicare and Medicaid costs; $180 million in mental health care for victims; $224 million in insurance claims processing; and $133 million for law enforcement and medic response to shooting injuries. In 2010, there were 36,341 emergency room visits and 25,024 hospitalizations for gun injuries, costing an estimated $6.3 million. Eighty-Four percent of those injured by firearms are uninsured, leaving taxpayers responsible for most of the bills through programs like Medicaid. According to the World Health Organization, the costs of gun violence can include legal services, medical costs, perpetrator control, policing, jailing, foster care, private security, lost earnings and time, life insurance, productivity, tourism, and psychological costs (pain and suffering), among others. The doubling of murder rates has been associated with a 12.5% decline in the value of neighborhood homes.

A LARGE PERCENTAGE OF AMERICANS, INCLUDING GUN OWNERS, SUPPORT MANY OF THE "COMMON SENSE" REGULATIONS REGARDING GUNS, SUCH AS THE BANNING OF HIGH CPACITY MAGAZINES, CRIMINAL BACKGROUND CHECKS, WAITING TIMES FOR GUN PURCHASES, PROFESSIONAL TRAINING, AND OTHER SUCH MEASURES. According to a Pew Research survey in March of 2013, 83% of all adults surveyed (and 79% of gun-owners; 86% of people living with a gun-owner; and

74% of NRA households) approve of background checks for private and gun show sales. About 40% of all gun sales are undocumented private party gun sales that do not require a background check, the often discussed "gun show loophole". Fifty-six percent of all adults surveyed approve of assault weapon bans and 53% of all adults surveyed approve of high-capacity magazine bans. Eighty-Nine percent of American adults with a gun in their homes are in favor of laws to prevent the purchase of guns by the mentally ill, and 82% approve of banning gun sales to people on no-fly lists. Don Macalady, member of Hunters against Gun Violence, stated, "As a hunter and someone who has owned guns since I was a young boy, I believe that commonsense gun legislation makes us all safer. Background checks prevent criminals and other dangerous people from getting guns."

FEWER SUICIDES OCCUR WHEN THERE IS MORE GUN CONTROL. Between 1999 and 2013 there were 270,237 firearm suicides in the United States, accounting for about 52% of all suicides during those years. According to a March 2014 study published in the *International Review of Law and Economics*, when gun ownership went down in the United States, overall suicide rates went down. Firearm-related suicides accounted for 61% of the gun deaths in the United States between 2000 and 2010. A study in December of 2009 published in *Health Policy*, found "general barrier to firearm access created through state regulation can have a significant deterrent effect on male suicide rates in the United States. Permit requirements and bans on sales to minors were the most effective of the regulations analyzed." A person who wants to kill him or herself is quite unlikely to commit suicide with poison or a knife, for example, when a gun is unavailable.

REGULATIONS REQUIRING SAFETY FEATURES CAN REDUCE GUN DEATHS. Approximately half of unintentional fatal shootings were self-inflicted; and family members or close friends caused most unintentional firearm deaths. According to the Law Center to Prevent Gun Violence and the National Physicians Alliance, states with the highest concentration of guns have nine times the amount of accidental gun deaths and "89% of unintentional shooting deaths of children occur in the home—and most of these deaths occur when children are playing with a loaded gun in their parents' absence." The nation's General Accounting Office (GAO) estimated that 31% of total accidental shooting deaths could have been prevented by installing safety devices on guns: 100% of deaths per year in which a child under 6 years old shoots and kills him/herself or another child could be prevented by automatic child-proof safety locks; and 23% of accidental shooting deaths by adolescents and adults per year could be prevented by loading indicators showing when a bullet was in the chamber ready to be fired. Marjorie Sanfilippo, PhD, Professor of Psychology at Eckerd College who has researched children's behavior around guns, stated, "We put gates around swimming pools to keep children from drowning. We put safety caps on medications to keep children from poisoning themselves… because children are naturally curious and impulsive, and because we have shown time and again that we cannot 'gun-proof' them with education, we have a responsibility to keep guns out of the hands of children."

THE AVAILABILITY OF GUNS MAKES VIOLENCE MORE LIKELY. The FBI found that in 2013 arguments (such as romantic triangles, brawls fueled by alcohol or drugs, and arguments over money) resulted in 1,962 gun deaths (59.9% of the total). [37] A June 1985 study published in the *American Journal of Public Health* found that "the weapons used [in altercations]… were those closest at hand." An editorial published in the June 1985 *American Journal of Public Health* noted, "gun-inflicted deaths [often] ensue from impromptu arguments and fights; in the US, two-thirds of the 7,900 deaths in 1981 involving arguments and brawls were caused by guns." A 1993 study published in *The New England Journal of Medicine* found that "rather than confer protection, guns kept in the home are associated with an increase in the risk of homicide by a family member or intimate acquaintance."

UNTRAINED ARMED CIVILIANS CAUSE MORE HARM THAN GOOD WHEN THEY TRY TO INTERVENE IN AN EMERGENCY SITUATION REGARDING A SHOOTER. *An armed civilian stopped none of the 62 mass shootings between 1982 and 2012.* Gun rights activists regularly state that a 2002 mass shooting at the Appalachian School of Law in Virginia was stopped by armed students, but those students were current and former law enforcement officers and the killer was out of bullets when stopped. Other mass shootings often held up as examples of armed citizens being able to stop mass shootings involved law enforcement or military personnel and/or the shooter had stopped shooting before being subdued, such as a 1997 high school shooting in Pearl, MS; a 1998 middle school dance shooting in Edinboro, PA; a 2007 church shooting in Colorado Springs, CO; and a 2008 bar shooting in Winnemucca, NV. Jeffrey Voccola, an Assistant Professor of Writing at Kutztown University, notes, "The average gun owner, no matter how responsible, is not trained in law enforcement or on how to handle life-threatening situations, so in most cases, if a threat occurs, increasing the number of guns only creates a more volatile and dangerous situation."

NATIONS WITH SERIOUS GUN REGULATION STATUTES HAVE LOWER MURDER AND SUICIDE RATES THAN THE UNITED STATES. Both Finland and Switzerland require gun owners to acquire licenses and pass background checks that include mental and criminal records, among other restrictions and requirements. In 2007 Switzerland ranked number 3 in international gun ownership rates with 45.7 guns per 100 people (about 3,400,000 guns total). In 2009 Switzerland had 24 gun homicides (0.31 deaths per 100,000 people) and 253 gun suicides (3.29 deaths per 100,000 people). Finland ranked fourth in international gun ownership rates with 45.3 guns per 100 people (about 2,400,000 guns total). In 2007 Finland had 23 (0.43 deaths per 100,000 people) gun homicides and 172 gun suicides (4.19 deaths per 100,000 people). The United States, categorized as having "permissive" firearm regulation by GunPolicy.org, ranked first in international gun ownership rates with 88.8 guns per 100 people (about 270,000,000 guns total). In 2007 the United States had 12,632 gun homicides (4.19 deaths per 100,000 people) and 17,352 gun suicides (5.76 deaths per 100,000 people). Harvard professor David Hemenway, PhD, wrote "We analyzed the relationship between homicide and gun availability using data from 26 developed countries from the early 1990s. We found that across developed countries, where guns are more available, there are more homicides." According to a March 2016 study, gun homicide rates in the United States were 25.3 times higher and gun suicides were 8 times higher in

2010 than in other populous, high-income countries. Additionally, 90% of women, 91% of 0- to 14-year olds, 92% of 15- to 24-year-olds, and 82% of all people killed by firearms were from the United States.

THE SECOND AMMENDEMENT WAS WRITTEN TO ALLOW MILITIAS TO BARE ARMS NOT INDIVIDUAL PEOPLE. Former Justice John Paul Stevens, JD, in his dissenting opinion for *District of Columbia et al. v. Heller*, wrote, "the Framer's single-minded focus in crafting the constitutional guarantee 'to keep and bear arms' was on military use of firearms, which they viewed in the context of service in state militias," hence the inclusion of the phrase "well regulated militia." Michael Waldman, JD, President of the Brennan Center for Justice at the New York University School of Law, stated there is nothing about an individual right to bear arms in the notes about the Second Amendment when it was being drafted, discussed, or ratified; the US Supreme Court declined to rule in favor of the individual right four times between 1876 and 1939; and all law articles on the Second Amendment from 1888 to 1959 stated that an individual right was not guaranteed.

CIVILIANS, HUNTERS INCLUDED, SHOULD NOT OWN MILITARY LEVEL WEAPONS. President Reagan and others did not think civilians should own the AR-15 military rifle and, when the AR-15 was included in the assault weapons ban of 1994 (which expired on September 13, 2004), the NRA actually supported the legislation. The Second Amendment was written at a time when the most common arms were long rifles that had to be reloaded after every shot. Civilians today have access to folding, detaching, or telescoping stocks that make the guns more easily concealed and carried; silencers to muffle gunshot sounds; flash suppressors to fire in low-light conditions without being blinded by the flash and to conceals the shooter's location; or grenade launcher attachments. Jonathan Lowy, Director of Legal Action Project at the Brady Center to Prevent Gun Violence, stated, "These are weapons that will shred your venison before you eat it, or go through the walls of your apartment when you're trying to defend yourself… they are made for mass killing, but not useful for law-abiding citizens."

Some ideas against gun control:

THERE ARE STILL MURDERS IN COUTIES WHERE HAND-GUNS ARE ILLEGAL. The UK outlawed handguns in 1997 after a man shot 16 elementary students and then killed himself. It is important to review the UK's homicide rate before, during, and after the ban… In 1996, the murder rate was 1.12 per 100,000 people. In 1997, it rose to 1.24. In 1998, the rate rose even further to 1.43. And in 2002, it peaked at 2.1 homicides per 100,000. Just because you ban guns, doesn't mean people won't find other ways to massacre others.

RESTRICTING ASSAULT RIFLES RESTRICT YOUR SECOND AMMENDMENT RIGHTS. If the government restricts the types of rifles or limits the amount of rounds, there's no limit to what else they may restrict. The infringement of your constitutional rights won't just stop at the type of arms you can own. Who knows what other rights they'll take away… free speech, freedom of religion, freedom of assembly, freedom of the press?

The Second Amendment is not intended for just ordinary home defense. Its intent was to guarantee the nation could never be overcome by any military power, foreign or domestic. If the military were not available… for example, a nuclear holocaust or a synchronized Pearl Harbor 9-11 occurred… you would need to protect yourself. If you were limited to non-assault rifles, any invader with an AK-47 would have an easy day.

AN ARMED CITIZENRY CAN HELP TAKE OUT THE BAD GUYS. For example, the first modern mass shooting in Austin, Texas in 1966. A sniper in a tower shot at university students for an hour and a half. The police who reacted had help. Students went to their trucks and grabbed their rifles and shot with the police. It was enough to pin the shooter down and allow the police to take the shooter out. Police then thanked the civilians for helping them fire on the shooter.

CRIMINALS WILL STILL GET GUNS, EVEN IF THEY ARE OUT-LAWED OR CONTOLLED. In 2009, a German high school student went on a rampage and killed 15 people. He did not have a gun. He used his father's 9 mm. Even in a country with strict gun laws, a shooter was able to find one and use it. **ABSOLUTE GUN RIGHTS CAN MAKE A POLICE STATE UNLIKELY.** Edward Snowden brought the abuse our constitutional rights to light. "Big Brother" is not a myth. It's a violation of the constitution. If the government doesn't protect your right, who or what will?

SHOOTERS PREFER SOFT TARGETS. They target elementary schools, and theaters, not places where people are likely to have guns.

PROHIBITION DID NOT WORK; IT WAS A FARCE THAT FED ORGANIZED CRIME. GUN CONTROL WOULD DO THE SAME. The people who prospered during Prohibition by importing and supplying alcohol were gangsters like Al Capone. If gun control were in place, the people we'd really have to worry about would be the modern-day Al Capone supplying guns.

CRIMINALS DO NOT OBEY LAWS. THIS PUTS THE LAW OBIDING CITIIZEN AT A REAL DISADVANTAGE. This is should be obvious. Gun control does not address the issue of gun-related crimes. In 2010, gun sales in Chicago were prohibited. There were 432 murders in 2010 and 500 in 2012. The FBI named Chicago the murder capital of America. If a criminal is going to break the law, they will easily find a way. That is what they do.

WE DO NOT LIVE IN A PERFECT WORLD PEOPLE!! You can't regulate it to perfection. There's about one gun for every citizen inside the United States already. Is it possible to call them all back? It would be impossible to collect this many guns or even a significant percentage of them. Even if the government wanted to, it could not control the guns already present... or guns that would find their way into those hands of those really want them.

Gun control has been, and probably will always be, a hot button issue. Unspeakable tragedies have led to little change, and powerful organizations and their money certainly have influence over our lawmakers. That said, it might be beneficial to at least study how other affluent free societies such as Japan, the UK, and Australia have dealt with this issue. We must also realize that there is a significant urban/rural divide in a vast nation such as ours.

If we viewed gun "control" as gun "regulation", perhaps training requirements, insurance requirements (One must insure their car in case they injure others), gun licensing (you must be licensed to drive a car, which also can be a deadly weapon), and gun sales (you have to pass title of a car on, and not a gun?) and gun identification (cars have VIN numbers, why can't guns be modified to only dispense bullets that can be traced back to that firearm?)

Finally, we must realize and probably accept that, for the most part, our legislator's are unwilling and unable to make changes. There are simply too many powerful forces that will make sure they will not have jobs if they even try. Gun control. Let's agree to disagree.

8

HATE CRIME

First, for purposes of our discussion, a definition of hate crime:

"A crime motivated by racial, sexual, or other prejudice, typically one involving violence."

What is controversial about hate crimes is not if they are good or bad. I like to think we all agree that they are bad. What is controversial is the existence of laws related to hate crimes, and increased sanctions against those that commit them.

Here are some of the arguments against hate crime penalties:

Hate crime laws are totally unneeded. All of the forbidden acts are already illegal and punishable.

Federal hate crime legislation gets the federal government far more involved in local activities and culture than they should be.

American justice is founded on the principle of all people being treated equally. If you punish someone more for a crime motivated by prejudice against a class protected by the hate crime legislation, and punish someone less for that same crime against a non-protected class, that is simply unfair. It is not equal justice under the law.

Hate crime legislation could limit an individual's freedom of speech. They may not be able to speak out against a group they do not like.

Hate crime legislation is political. It gives political power to groups engaging in behaviors others might find objectionable.

Hate crime laws give protected class status to people that are not deserving. No one should be a " protected class".

Hate crime legislation is put into effect by legislators that are seeking to be politically correct and are trolling for votes.

Some arguments for hate crime legislation:

Hate crime laws are essential because a hate crime is not committed against just a single individual. All people in that class are terrorized by an action taken against someone simply because of their religion, race, or sexual orientation. Therefore, they are fair and necessary in a moral society.

Federal hate crime legislation helps local people. Sometimes local communities do not have the will or resources to protect a class of people subject to discrimination, prejudice, or violence.

Hate crime legislation may help make the public aware of a group subject to discrimination or abuse. This awareness can have a protective effect.

In the past, Civil Rights legislation decreased bigotry, discrimination, and violence against minorities. Hate crime laws might also provide such protections for other groups.

Such legislation also could protect women, the disabled, the elderly, not just transgender or homosexual people.

Some people just oppose hate crime laws. Why? How can someone be against laws that protect people from being targeted because of their race, ethnicity, religion, nationality, disabilities, gender identity or sexual orientation?

Here's how: Some folks oppose hate crime laws because they say the feel they are unnecessary and redundant. They say that we already have laws against assault and murder, so we do not need laws against assault and murder motivated by hate. This is their thought process, but is it correct? The purpose of laws is to deter and punish antisocial behavior, behavior that violates the rights of people. Hate crime laws impose additional penalties for crimes motivated by hate, and this provides deterrence. I suggest that most haters who assault or murder people out of hatred for the group they belong to would not commit the crimes of assault or murder to steal a wallet, or hijack a car. They're not muggers or thieves intent on stealing something of monetary value from another human being. They don't care about your wallet or car. They want to hurt you or kill you because you're black or Islamic or gay or transgender. They don't know you, but they don't like the group you belong to, so they want to harm you or even kill you. Their violent crime is not a means to an end — getting your wallet — but an end in and of itself — specifically, getting you. If they are deterred from acting out their hatred, they are unlikely ever to engage in a violent criminal act at all.

We may have to agree to disagree on hate crime legislation. But we can all agree that crime and hate are wrong.

9

IMMIGRATION (ILLEGAL)

—

One of the most controversial topics today, and throughout our history, is immigration. In this chapter we will discuss illegal immigration.

It is estimated that the United States is home to approximately 11 million immigrants that are here illegally. Immigration is always a heated and potentially divisive debate.

Many see illegal immigration as a positive for our society. Illegal immigrants pay taxes, and this increases our national welfare. Illegal immigrants often take jobs that few if any others will take. These jobs are essential to our high standard of living, and the lower wages paid to immigrants lower prices for all of us. Immigrants, more often than not, come here to work. They work hard at lower wage but essential jobs.

Those that oppose illegal immigration often believe that people that broke the law, whether they overstayed a visa, or crossed the border illegally, should be deported. They are, after all, criminals. They broke the law. They certainly should not be rewarded with a path to citizenship. These "illegal's" drain social services and are burdens, it is believed.

It is important to define some terms using " governmentese":

1. Immigrant

An alien who has been granted the right by the USCIS to reside permanently in the United States and to work without restrictions in the United States. Also known as a Lawful Permanent Resident (LPR). All immigrants are eventually issued a "green card" (USCIS Form I-551), which is the evidence of the alien's LPR status. LPR's who are awaiting the issuance of their green cards may bear an I-551 stamp in their foreign passports.

Immigrant visas are available for aliens (and their spouses and children) who seek to immigrate based on their job skills. If an alien has the right combination of skills, education, and/or work experience and are otherwise eligible; the alien may be able to live permanently in the United States. Per USCIS, there are five employment-based immigrant visa preferences (categories): EB-1, EB-2, EB-3, EB-4 and EB-5.

2. Nonimmigrant

An alien who has been granted the right by the USCIS to reside temporarily in the United States. Each nonimmigrant is admitted into the United States in the nonimmigrant status, which corresponds to the class of visa with which, or purpose for which, he entered the United States (e.g., a foreign student may enter the United States on an F-1 visa, which corresponds to the F-1 student status in which he was admitted to the United States).

Aliens in some nonimmigrant statuses are allowed to be employed in the United States, and others are not. Some nonimmigrant statuses have rigid time limits for the alien's stay in the United States, while others do not.

Each nonimmigrant status has rules and guidelines, which must be followed in order for the nonimmigrant to remain "in status." A nonimmigrant that violates one of these rules or guidelines will fall "out of status." An nonimmigrant who remains "out of status" for at least 180 days is deportable and will be unable to re-enter the United States for 3 years. A nonimmigrant who remains "out of status" for at least 365 days is deportable and will be unable to re-enter the United States for 10 years.

3. Illegal Alien

Also known as an "Undocumented Alien," is an alien who has entered the United States illegally and is deportable if apprehended, or an alien who entered the United States legally but who has fallen "out of status" and is deportable.

4. Nonimmigrant Visas

A nonimmigrant visa allows a nonimmigrant to enter the United States in one of several different categories, which correspond to the purpose for which the nonimmigrant is being admitted to the United States. For example, a foreign student will usually enter the United States on an F-1 visa, a visitor for business on a B-1 visa, an exchange visitor (including students, teachers, researchers, trainees, alien physicians, au pairs, and others) on a J-1 visa, a diplomat on an A or G visa, etc. The categories of nonimmigrant visas correspond exactly to the "nonimmigrant status" assigned to each nonimmigrant upon his arrival, based on the purpose for which the nonimmigrant was admitted to the United States. For example, a foreign student who enters the United States on an F-1 visa is considered to be in F-1 student status after he enters the United States; and he will remain in that status until he violates the conditions prescribed for that status, or until he changes to another nonimmigrant or immigrant status with USCIS permission, or until he leaves the United States.

An undocumented or "illegal alien" is an alien who entered the United States illegally without the proper authorization and documents, or is an alien who once entered the United States legally and has since violated the terms of the status in which he entered the United States or has overstayed the time limits of his original status.

Approximately 95% of the foreign academic students in the United States have entered the country on F-1 (student) or J-1 (Exchange Visitor) visas. Foreign vocational students usually enter the United States on M-1 visas. Foreign students and faculty members might also enter the United States on Q (Cultural Exchange Visitor) visas; however, the numbers who do so is small. A large number of foreign teachers and researchers have entered the United States on J-1 (Exchange Visitor) visas; but a great many of the foreign faculty members have also entered the United States on H-1b visas (Specialty Occupation), O-1 visas (Alien with Extraordinary Ability), and TN visas (NAFTA Professional from Canada or Mexico).

Most students in F-1 or J-1 status have no specific time limits imposed on their stay in the United States (evidenced by the notation D/S (Duration of Status) on their immigration Form I-94), while aliens in most other nonimmigrant statuses have various time limits imposed on their stay in the United States. Aliens in some nonimmigrant statuses are allowed to be employed in the United States, while nonimmigrant in other statuses are not. Nonimmigrant's who are allowed to be employed in the United States can usually get a United States social security number.

Foreign Students in F-1 or J-1 status are usually allowed to be employed for no more than 20 hours per week during the academic year, but are allowed to work 40 hours per week during the summer and other vacations. Certain students may be allowed to work off campus with permission from USCIS or from the Designated School Official (usually the foreign student advisor). Certain students in hardship situations are issued Employment Authorization Documents (EAD) and are allowed to work off campus with no hour limitations. F-1 students are allowed to be employed for a maximum of 12 months in "practical training" jobs both on and off campus. These are jobs, which are related to the student's subject area of study.

5. Visa Waiver Program (VWP)

The Visa Waiver Program (VWP) enables citizens of participating countries to travel to the United States for tourism or business for 90 days or less without obtaining a United States visa. The Attorney General in consultation with the Secretary of State administers the VWP. The Visa Waiver Program (VWP) was created by an act of Congress as a pilot program in 1986 and implemented in 1988. Congress passed legislation to make the program permanent in October 2000, and the President signed the legislation on October 30, 2000.

Illegal immigrants that are granted " legal status", a debate we are currently having, would bring about the following changes:

1. Illegal immigrants granted legal status would no longer be subject to deportation only because they're in the country illegally, as long as they are law abiding in other ways.
2. They would be allowed to work legally and above board.
3. They would be able travel in and out of the United States. At least 60 percent of the illegal population has been in the United States for more than a decade and are unable to return to their home countries to visit family.
4. A "path to citizenship for illegal "immigrants" means that as naturalized citizens, they would be eligible to receive government benefits, such as unemployment insurance, Workman's Compensation and Social Security. They could potentially vote. They would also be eligible for special immigration privileges, such as being able to bring family members into the country. If they were to commit a crime, they can not be deported

There are some interesting things about illegal immigration that we need to be aware of:

The number of illegal immigrants living in the United States was lower in 2015 than it was at the end of the Great Recession in 2009. The origin countries of unauthorized immigrants also shifted during that time, with the number from Mexico declining.

Some interesting facts about the illegal immigrant population in the United States:

1. There were 11 million unauthorized immigrants in the U.S. in 2015, a small but statistically significant decline from the Pews Center's estimate of 11.3 million for 2009.

The Center's preliminary estimate of the unauthorized immigrant population in 2016 is 11.3 million, which is statistically no different from the 2009 or 2015 estimates because it is based on a data source with a smaller sample size and larger margin of error. Unauthorized immigrants represented 3.4% of the total U.S. population in 2015. The number of unauthorized immigrants peaked in 2007 at 12.2 million, when this group was 4% of the U.S. population.

2. **Mexicans may no longer be the majority of unauthorized immigrants in the United States.** They made up half of all unauthorized immigrants in 2016, according to the Center's <u>preliminary estimate</u>, marking the first time in at least a decade that they did not account for a clear majority of this population. Their numbers (and share of the total) have been declining in recent years: There were 5.6 million Mexican unauthorized immigrants living in the U.S. in 2015 and 2016, down from 6.4 million in 2009.

Meanwhile, the number of unauthorized immigrants from nations other than Mexico has grown since 2009, from 5 million that year to 5.4 million in 2015. Non-Mexicans numbered 5.7 million in the preliminary 2016 estimate, a total that was not statistically different from 2015.

From 2009 to 2015, the number of unauthorized immigrants from Asia and Central America rose. Increases in the number from other countries have mostly offset the decline in the number from Mexico (and a relatively small decrease in the number from South America).

An interesting phenomenon of recent times is birth tourism. Pregnant women from other nations will travel to the United States as "tourists". Their intent is to have their children born in the United States because we have birth right citizenship. If you are born here you are a citizen. This gives the parents peace of mind if things become difficult in their home country. Their child is a US citizen and can always come here. And even bring family in many cases. Also, if the child has no intention of coming here to live, they can come as a student, and, as a US citizen, have a better chance of being admitted into an American college.

We are certainly a nation of laws. That is one of the major reasons people from all over the world want to come here. Certainly, this gives us a leg up on many other nations. We are also a nation of compassion. We have people here that were brought here at a very young age by their parents. Their parents came here illegally. These people are not US citizens because they were not born here. Our country is the only country they have ever known. Though not US citizens, they are truly American. Are these people to be sent away, deported? We are a nation of laws. We are also compassionate. People have strong opinions on what to do, especially with people that arrived here as babies and have lived here decades and contributed. Do we agree to disagree?

Is there a solution that is both compassionate and respecting of the rule of law? This debate will continue.

We have had a history of periodically restricting certain groups. Those restrictions are stopped, and another group is looked at with skepticism. Most people that come here assimilate; they came here because they wanted to become Americans. Yet, we all have pride in our ancestor whether we are of Irish, Polish, Mexican, or Chinese heritage. We are a hyphenated people, a nation of immigrants, but in the end, all Americans.

10

JAIL

—

America flat out locks up a lot of folks. So many, that public prisons cannot seem to hold all of those prisoners. Sociologists tell us there are five purposes for incarceration:

1. Punishment-A just society must punish wrongdoers.
2. Deterrence-prison time deters criminal wrongdoing,
3. Protection-We are a lot safer if the bad guys are locked up.
4. Rehabilitation-Criminals should be rehabilitated in prison, so that they can contribute to society when released.
5. No other options-Sometimes, especially with repeat/serious offenders, we have run out of ways to deal with them.

Here is the controversial question of the day. Should we have privately run for profit prisons?

Here are some pros and cons-

Pros of Private Prisons:

1. Private prisons may save taxpayers money.
A private prison industry can seek lower prices for necessary components of a prison and cut costs. Private business is better at that than government. . A private business can often make changes quicker than a government agency, improve operational efficiencies, and implement cost-savings measures. A private prison industry reduces the size of government because operational responsibilities shift to the private institution, which may reduce taxpayer costs.

2. Local communities will benefit from private for profit prisons.
Communities that have private prisons operating within their boundaries often receive new tax revenues, have new jobs to provide local people, and this creates more spending for the support ofbusinesses in that area.

3. Prisoner population levels are more appropriately maintained.
Many public prison systems are operating at a capacity that is much higher than originally intended. In California, for example, the public prison system was operating at 137.5% of capacity before the Supreme Court required the state to begin reducing overcrowding. Private prisons can better control population levels by transporting prisoners to specific locations where there are greater needs. This lessens the threat of overcrowding to local systems while still allowing for profitability.

4. Private prisons may lower the rates of recidivism.
A study of a private prison in Arkansas tracked over 650 women who were released after they completed a re-entry program. After 5 years, only 1 in 5 of the women being tracked had committed another criminal offense. This means that private prisons have the potential to lower the rates of repeat offenders by up to 50% in some areas.

5. Facilities can be used for various purposes.
Many private prisons are today being used for immigration housing and detention purposes. They can also be retrofitted to serve a variety of community needs if the need for a prison goes away. This allows for the investments that a community provides to not be in vain should prisoner levels not be as high as anticipated.

6. Governments have contracted prisoners out to third parties for several years.
This practice is not new. Specific services for the public prison system have been contracted out to private businesses for more than a century. This includes inmate transportation, food preparation, medical services, and even vocational training. These structures easily transition over to the management and operations of the entire prison. Private prisons have been in place with the modern US criminal justice system since 1984, when Corrections Corporation of America was awarded their first operational contract.

Cons of Private Prisons:

1. Prisoners tend to serve longer sentences in private prisons.

Studies from the University of Wisconsin system have shown that prisoners who are being held in private prisons may serve sentences that are up to 7% longer than prisoners who are in public prisons serving a similar sentence. This is directly correlated to the profit-potential that each prisoner provides the organization that is overseeing the incarceration. Private prisons may find reasons (prisoner misbehavior, etc) to keep prisoners longer because each prisoner represents profit. If prosecutors and judges invest in a private prison directly or indirectly, is this not a serious conflict of interest?

2. Many private prisons do not house costly prisoners.

Many private prisons are given the opportunity to pick and choose which prisoners they house. whereas taxpayer operated prisons take all comers. High-risk prisoners tend to be costlier to supervise, which means they have a higher cost to the business. These costly prisoners are shipped back to public prisons, hitting taxpayers with the cost while the private prison profits off the low maintenance prisoners. A study by the US Bureau of Justice Statistics found that Arizona public facilities were 7 times more likely to house a violent offender a 3 times more likely to house an inmate convicted of a serious offense compared to private prisons in the area. This suggests that private prisons are either incapable or unwilling to do the job, in its full measure, as compared to public prisons.

3. Private prisons can leave communities with costly facilities that are empty.

Private prisons are operated on a contractual basis. The community is often responsible for the facility, because they may have offered incentives to the private prison to locate there. The private prison is responsible for filling the beds. If the private prison sees no profit in continuing the operation, they can close their doors and stick a community with an empty facility, no jobs, and the bills that remain for the initial construction.

4. Private prisons tend to be more violent because of low staffing levels. Staff levels are low because they are trying to maximize profits

Private prisons have up to 50% more violence when compared to public prisons with regards to inmate-on-officer assaults. For-profit facilities also see over 60% more inmate-on-inmate assaults. Such assaults may lead to more prison time, and more profit for the facility. This is often due to low officer staffing levels that are in private facilities. Some officer-to-prisoner ratios in private prisons can exceed 1 officer to every 120 prisoners.

5. Prisoners can be thousands of miles away from their family. The prisons are located based on profit potential reason for the business; the needs of the inmates and their families may receive little consideration.

Prisoner exchange programs can cause inmate transfers that may be hundreds, if not thousands, of miles away from their family. This removes the prisoner from their network of support, forcing them to rely on internal systems to meet their needs. This creates more barriers to rehabilitation, making the private prison more about housing prisoners and less about bringing them back into society as a productive member. It is mostly about profit.

6. There is more incentive for corruption.

Because prisoners are required for a private prison to be profitable, their budgets are never 100% certain. To solve this problem, there are several instances of corporations working with local systems of justice to extend sentences to longer lengths or charge with higher-level crimes for longer sentences.

7. Employee wages are often lower and there are often fewer benefits.

One of the ways that the private prison system saves money is by providing employees with lower wages and fewer benefits than employees in the public prison system. Correctional officers in the public system can earn up to $75,000 per year. In comparison, many correctional officers in the private system may earn as little as $14 per hour. Is this in the best interest of society, the prisoners, or the rehabilitation goal of imprisonment?

8. There may not be any real cost-savings advantages.
Comparisons of private v public prisons that are of similar size and house similar inmates show that both systems face similar cost-per-day rates, despite the fact that private institutions often pay lower wages and employ fewer workers.

The advantages and disadvantages of private prisons involve cost, efficiency, and effectiveness. When a private prison is operating with best practices and focused on rehabilitation, it can be a beneficial addition to a community. Unfortunately, many corporations are focusing on profits over purpose, which can create numerous disadvantages to the prisoners and society.

We may all agree that prisons should punish, deter, protect society, and rehabilitate criminals. Are for profit prisons incentivized to rehabilitate, when they may make a larger profit if the prisoner that is released reoffends?

Private v public services are always debated; this debate has extended to the prison industry. We may have to agree to disagree as to the appropriateness of for profit prisons.

II

KEYNESIAN ECONOMICS

—

Debt is a bad thing? Right? Buy a home, and most people are in debt.

They have a mortgage. But isn't debt bad? You want to attend college. You take out loans. You earn a degree. But now you are in debt for a long time. But we've agreed debt is bad. Perhaps there are shades of gray for an individual.

Maybe there is such a thing as good debt and bad debt. Maybe the concept of good debt and bad debt applies to nations.

Whether or not a nation should ever be in debt is an area of controversy that has raged the entire time there has been a United States. To understand debt, and whether or not it is a good thing or a bad thing for a nation, we should probably discuss something called Keynesian Economics.

Keynesian Economics is an economic theory of total spending in the economy and its effects on output and inflation. The British Economist John Maynard Keynes developed his theory during the 1930s in an effort to understand the Great Depression. Keynes advocated for increased government expenditures and lower taxes to stimulate demand and pull the global economy out of the Depression.

Since that time the term "Keynesian economics" has referred to the concept that optimal economic performance could be achieved – and economic slumps prevented – by influencing aggregate demand through an activist stabilization and economic intervention policies by the government. Keynesian economics is considered to be a "demand-side" theory that focuses on changes in the economy over the short term.

Before Keynesian economics was postulated, classical economic thinking held that cyclical swings in employment and economic output would be modest and that they would are "self adjusting". According to this classical theory, if aggregate demand in the economy fell, the resulting weakness in production and jobs would precipitate a decline in prices and wages. A lower level of inflation and wages would induce employers to make capital investments in their businesses and employ more people, stimulating employment and restoring economic growth.

The depth and severity of the Great Depression, however, severely tested this hypothesis. People's lives were at stake. Keynes maintained in his seminal book, "General Theory of Employment, Interest and Money," and other writings, that structural rigidities and certain characteristics of market economies would exacerbate economic weakness and cause aggregate demand to plunge even further.

As an example, Keynesian economics dismisses the belief held by some economists that lower wages can restore full employment, by arguing that employers will not add employees to produce goods that cannot be sold because demand is weak. Similarly, poor business conditions may cause companies to reduce capital investment, rather than take advantage of lower prices to invest in new plant and equipment; this would also have the effect of reducing overall expenditures and employment.

The global financial crisis of 2007–08 "The Great Recession" caused resurgence in Keynesian ideas. It was the theoretical underpinnings of economic policies in response to the crisis by many governments, including in our nation as well as the United Kingdom. As the global recession was beginning in late 2008, Harvard professor N. Gregory Mankiw wrote in the *New York Times*, "If you were going to turn to only one economist to understand the problems facing the economy, there is little doubt that the economist would be John Maynard Keynes." Although Keynes died more than a half-century ago, his diagnosis of recessions and depressions remains the foundation of modern macroeconomics. Keynes wrote, 'Practical men, who believe themselves to be quite exempt from any intellectual influence, are usually the slave of some defunct economist.' In 2008, no defunct economist is more prominent than Keynes himself."

But the 2007–08 disasters also showed that Keynesian theory should include the role of the financial system. Keynesian economists are rectifying that omission by integrating the real and financial sectors of the economy.

Pro Keynesian:
China became a Keynesian nation by spending on infrastructure investment to avoid as recession from 2008 through 2016. They were quite successful maintaining growth throughout what was a recession for most of the world.

China has continued to use government fiscal spending to stimulate the economy and avert the ill effects the rest of the planet is experiencing from the fall out of the 2008 Great Recession. Government spending of cash reserves and significant increases in governmental debt though real fuels this economic growth. Recovery through fiscal stimulus is something the United States failed to do in earnest during the Great Recession though in the Great Depression the US efforts in this regard significantly helped the economy. Some moderation between the Chinese and US responses to the Great Recession is probably economically most favorable.

Now China has too much debt and the US has too little stimulus. Though China's economic stimulus program is commendable and forward looking as it has built a lot of infrastructure for immediate and future use (over built), as we know there is a point where debt becomes a limiting issue reducing future economic flexibility and eating up current fiscal budgets.

Con Keynesian:

What may be considered a good argument against Keynesian economics it that it takes a measure of restraint during more prosperous times. As the economy shifts into an upturn, taxes should be collected and used to pay down the debts created during slower times. Good times is not a time to cut taxes or spend more, it may even be the best time to increase taxes and spend less thus paying off the debt created during the hard times at a faster rate than inactive management of the economy would produce.

Unfortunately such restrain is rare.

So Keynesian Economics might boil down to this question: should the government get highly involved in the economy to help smooth it out, especially during the hard times? If that smoothing helps you, you might be answering in the affirmative to that question. This is another area where we may have to agree to disagree. There will always be an argument about small government v large government.

12

LONGER SCHOOL YEAR

—

The length of the American school year has been debated from the early days of our nation to the present. Why do we not have as many school days each school year as many other nations have? Is this shortfall a determent to our kids? To our country? There are loud voices in this debate. Is this issue solvable?

Let us look at some school day per year comparisons by nation:

Japan	243
West Germany	266-240
South Korea	220
Israel	216
Luxembourg	216
Soviet Union	211
Netherlands	200
Scotland	200
Thailand	200
Hong Kong	195
England/Wales	192
Hungary	192
Switzerland	191
Finland	190
New Zealand	
Nigeria	
British Columbia	
France	
Ontario	
Ireland	
New Brunswick	
Quebec	
Spain	
Sweden	
United States	
French Belgium	
Flemish Belgium	

"Repairing" the educational system has long been a focus of attention by educational experts and the public for a long time. But too often the "repair" has been a silver-bullet solution that has garnered small outcomes at best and occasionally drawn worse outcomes than if no bullet had been fired at all. The last couple of decades have seen there share of experiments with standardized testing, charter schools, vouchers, private schooling, and reducing class size experiments all with questionable results from an outcomes and return on investment perspective.

Longer school years are not a magic bullet, but it is one idea that may be promising. For the 14 wealthy countries studied in *Measure of a Nation*, the data show clearly that there is a correlation of about ninety percent between the numbers of days a child attends school and the PISA exam scores (the PISA exams are a worldwide evaluation of 15-year-old pupils' scholastic performance in math, science, and reading). Although correlation doesn't mean causation, as we all know, the strength of the relationship seen in a graph of this relationship does seem to support the logic of more days in schools leading to better performance, so it becomes hard to resist arguing that a longer school year would improve American academic performance. After all, the relationship is intuitive; as nearly every teacher will tell you, the long summer break sets children far behind in their learning. Research certainly supports this notion.

In our American schools there are *no* national standards for the length of the school year. Rather, this decision is left up to the individual states. It is a different story altogether in most other nations. A majority of states require a minimum school year of 180 days; ten states require fewer than 180 days; and one state, Minnesota, has no minimum requirement for either the days of the school year or the hours of instruction. The American minimums are in stark contrast to the 220 days averaged by top-performing South Korea and the 201 days in Japan, also a top performer. It seems obvious that 20 percent more days of school provide more exposure to educational materials.

More generally, the long summer vacation typical of the American school year is not beneficial for student education, although it may be highly beneficial for some industries — tourism, summer camps, airlines — which rely on the long summer vacation for much of their revenue. American students typically are given ten weeks off for the summer, plenty of time to regress in their knowledge and study habits. Forgetting curves, developed in the late nineteenth century by German psychologist Hermann Ebbinghaus, demonstrate that memory retention declines exponentially over time, so the long American summer vacation takes a major toll on a student's ability to progress. This science is indisputable.

The recommendation of a longer school year for American students is not new. The US Department of Education made the recommendation in 1992, and President Obama repeated the call for longer school days and school years in September 2010, during an interview on a television morning show. Some charter schools, a concept that is gaining steam, have implemented more classroom time. The Knowledge Is Power Program (KIPP) academies, typically established in inner-city school districts, mandate some 60 percent more classroom time than traditional programs and add half-day classes twice a month. To add another month of school would require major changes to take place not only in our educational system but also changes in many of the for-profit industries (that have formidable lobbying power) that were mentioned above.

Longer school years are not a silver bullet, but they are one of the leading practices found in other countries that are excelling at primary and secondary education. Other leading practices include selecting top talent to become teachers, paying teachers well (to attract that talent), investing in ongoing teacher development (resulting in minimal turnover), making teaching a prestigious position, equalizing funding for education (so poorer students had similar educational opportunities as students from wealthier communities) and increasing enrollment in pre-primary education.

A good foundation of early pre-school learning is an investment that pays for itself many times over.

Do schools have summers off because of the agrarian roots of our nation? There is a kernel of truth to this (corny pun intended).

Earlier in history what school on the agrarian calendar actually looked like was a short winter term and a short summer term. If one thinks about farming needs, that's actually what makes sense.

Children in rural, agricultural areas were most needed in the spring, when most crops had to be planted, and in the fall, when crops were harvested and sold. Historically, many attended school in the summer when there was comparatively less need for them on the farm.

The whole concept of an agrarian calendar makes it sound like it was an unthinking decision but the current school year was really a conscious creation.

Our urban schools had a very different school schedule, but also routinely included summer. School was essentially open year round, but was not mandatory, and children came when they could. In 1842, New York City schools were open 248 days a year, dramatically more than the 180 or so that they are open present day .

In the pre- air conditioning era, schools and entire cities could be sweltering places during the hot summer months. Wealthy and eventually middle-class urbanites also usually made plans to flee the city's heat, making those months the logical time in cities to suspend school.

By the late 19th century, school reformers started pushing for A standardization of the school calendar across urban and rural areas. So a compromise was struck that created the modern school calendar.

A long break would give teachers needed time to train and give children a rest. And while summer was the logical time to take off, the cycles of farming had precious little to do with it.

And none of the reasons for creating the current school calendar related to student achievement. The dialog that we're having today about creating a context for academic achievement just weren't there.

Today researchers are considering that exact question.

Long summer breaks have been shown to cause children, especially lower-income children, to lose ground academically. It's a phenomenon known as "summer slide," where students return to school in the fall having lost a full month of learning, on average.

Researchers have also studied enrichment summer programs, summer school, and even year-round school to combat this summer learning loss. One school district in West Virginia has had a year-round calendar for more than two decades.

So, we know that many students loose knowledge over the long summer break. We also know that there are no agricultural reasons for the long summer vacation, and never really were. Students, parents, and teachers are used to long breaks. Many do not want to give them up. Many industries depend on that long break for a significant portion of their profits. And yes, even Congress takes a summer break.

Is this tradition, as antiquated as it is, the best thing?

Perhaps we may have to agree to disagree.

13

MEDIOCRITY

—

We are a nation of sports fans. Mediocrity of the teams we follow seems to be valued.

Parity is the new ideal in professional sports. Ownership wants all teams to have a chance to win the championship in any given year. I think the NFL started this mantra with its " Any given Sunday" philosophy. The NFL would be happy to have 32 eight and eight teams at seasons end. The fans seem to clamor for this too. We all want uniform mediocrity, and no great teams.

The NBA and NHL are no different. Salary caps and other restrictions have made prolonged dominance and greatness a phenomenon of the past. No team should have a multi-year run. No more " six-peats". Prolonged excellence has been legislated away by the owners, aided and abetted by the fans, the ones, by the way, that are footing the bills. Are they just giving us what we think we want, or are they just trying to make huge amounts of money?

When I was a little Chicago sports fan, and the Cubs were always out of contention by mid April, had no lights, and you could only see day baseball, there were dominant teams. You knew certain teams were going to come into town and just hand the Cubbies their heads. On the South Side, you knew the Yankees were going to come into town and just destroy the Pale Hose. These dominant teams did not kill your love of baseball. In fact, you loved it more. There is nothing more exciting than a David Versus Goliath story.

Beyond this, excellence and dominance as a group was something to be admired, and aspired to. Lousy teams in cow towns all dreamed of the day they would become the Montreal Canadians, the Green Bay Packers, or New York Yankees.

Now, excellence and success are punished. If your team wins the Stanley Cup, the salary cap makes sure the players are not rewarded for their effort. They must be shipped off to the likes of Columbus or Dallas (why are there even hockey teams in Texas?) so that those cities can hoist the cup as well.

I long for the days when excellence was rewarded. An organization could go on an extended run, the players could be rewarded and not moved out for their sacrifices, even if it meant a visiting team would come in year after year and kick our hinnies. One year, through *honest* effort, and not salary cap limits, it might be us.

I miss the days of being able to knock off Goliath, and not have a " participation" trophy given to us.

Young people do learn values from sports, and are motivated by sports. Do we want them to think that everyone will get their turn, regardless of talent?

When I was knee high to a major league shortstop, each league sent only ONE team to the post season. People still loved the game; it was " Americas' Pastime". Prolonged excellence of a team was not reviled. There was no expectation that every team should get its turn.

If excellence and talent should not determine a teams quality, if every dog should have their day, let us just decide the Cubbies should be awarded the World Series next year whether they earn it or not. Heavens knows it's about time; they have won only one this century.

Twenty years ago my daughters last placed softball team received a huge trophy. My daughter asked why they deserved it; she said, " We stunk".

If sports are a metaphor for society, do we not want excellence rewarded? In the real world, is everyone a winner?

Is it better to have a league of fifteen mediocre teams, all of which have a shot at glory, or a league of 14 mediocre teams and one great team? Should success be punished (lower draft Picks, having to let players go because of salary cap limitations)? Does this press for competitiveness, giving every team or entity a turn, even if it means hurting the successful group, stretch into other areas of our culture? If so, is that a good thing?

The debate goes on. We may have to agree to disagree. This much is certain: The Cubs have reached their quota.

14

NATIONAL PARKS

—

As hard as it may be to believe, there is some controversy about national parks. Do we have too many? Are they too big?

First, we will take a look at where they are, and when they were established:

Some are against national parks, or at least expansion of national parks because they believe that states should have control of their lands, not the federal government. It is often viewed as federal government overreach. Others oppose national parks because the land cannot be exploited, mined, used for profit, etc.

There are advantages to national parks:

National parks are large areas of public land set aside for native plants, animals and the places in which they thrive. **National parks** are home to many endemic species. They also protect places **important** to the original Americans, and are places that show how people lived in the past. **National parks** are protected areas.

National parks often contain **wildlife sanctuaries**, and protected spaces for nature help conserve the natural world and benefit mankind in numerous ways. A National Park not only gives someone a place to walk and exercise, and a **wildlife sanctuary** promotes conservation, both of which play an important role in society.

Conservation of biodiversity (the variety of our native species and the ecosystems they form) is the central purpose of many national parks. High levels of biodiversity keep ecosystems healthy and resilient, which means that they continue providing vital ecosystem services such as nutrient cycling, climate regulation, air and water purification and pollination.

Protecting biodiversity is vital to safeguard the economy; our cultural, spiritual and aesthetic values; and the intrinsic value of species and ecosystems. National parks provide a safe home for native plants and animals. They help keep the air and water clean. National parks give us places to enjoy.

National parks help us to learn about the environment, history and wild life.

The world's first national park was established by an act of Congress in 1872 as a "pleasuring ground for the benefit and enjoyment of the people in order to protect for all time this outstanding natural area.

We need fresh air, clean water and healthy food. Without them we would suffer. The leaves of plants make fresh air. Their roots hold the soil together, which stops erosion and helps keep our waterways clean. National parks have lots of plants so they play a big part in keeping our environment healthy.

National parks are places for people to relax in and enjoy. There are lots of things to do in a national park such as swimming, skiing, painting, mountaineering, taking photographs, enjoying the view and taking in fresh air.

National parks are places for everybody to learn about native plants and animals and the way they rely on each other. Historic sites and Aboriginal sites also help us to learn about how people lived in the past.

National parks are a way to safeguard our history for future generations.

In a sense, national parks are more for our grandchildren and great grandchildren than they are for us.

There are also arguments against national parks:

National parks, in the eyes of some, hurt the economy. If owned by the private sector, they could become theme parks, provide a lot of jobs, and generate a lot of tax revenue. Now, they simply use tax dollars. National parks, if privately owned, could be exploited for mineral wealth.

Having visited national parks I can tell you that there are often many foreigners there. Often, they out number Americans. They seem quite jealous that we have these places.

National parks have entered the debate involving national v local control, government overreach, and public v private ownership and management.

We can agree to disagree. Lets just keep the ones we have and have our theme parks and mining elsewhere.

15

OBSTRUCTIONISM

—

The dictionary defines obstructionism as: "the practice of deliberately impeding or delaying the course of legal, legislative, or other procedures".

I think we would all agree that we are living in an era of obstructionism. Members of Congress (the House and the Senate) proudly tout their willingness to make sure nothing gets done if they do not get what they desire. Even a minority, less than 50 percent, can stop laws from being made. The phrase " elections have consequences" may no longer mean anything. If the party of which you are a member looses an election, you can still grind the wheels of government to a halt, if things are not going the way you want them to.

There is disagreement on this point, however-is obstructionism good or bad?

If you believe you should never give in when your principles are at stake, even if nothing at all can be accomplished, then obstructionism is good. If you believe that you can get 99 percent of what you think is good for the country, and have to swallow one thing that is not, you are against obstructionism.

Voltaire once made this statement: "Don't let the perfect be the enemy of the good." In other words, instead of pushing things to an impossible "perfect," and therefore getting nowhere, accept "good." Many things worth doing are worth doing badly

As one can see, it appears as though less may be getting finished in terms of laws being passed. Is obstructionism to blame?

In our current times, if one party does not like another party's nominee for a judgeship, they will utilize parliamentary procedures to make sure the nominee does not even get a vote as to their confirmation. Is this good or bad? If you have strong beliefs and believe in no compromising, this is a good thing. If you believe in compromise perhaps obstructionism is bad, we may have to agree to disagree on this. Let's just not put it up to a vote.

16

POLICE

—

Do we have enough police? Do we have too many? Are they good, or bad? What kinds of police do we have?

Have police overstepped their roles?

Like any other profession (including doctors, lawyers, dentists, teachers, architects, clergy, and so on) the police have a small percentage of " bad apples". Most probably a much smaller percentage than most professions. As they are among the few professions sanctioned to take lives in our name (the military being the other) they are held to the very highest of standards. Because their work is so important to our society (we would not have one without them) their actions are magnified. More often than not, their mistakes are what we see the talking heads on television discussing. Their heroism, good everyday actions, is less seldom reported. When we get a ticket, we hate cops. When we need them, we NEED them.

How many cops are there in the United States? In 2008, the last year relatively good statistics were available, according to the Bureau of Justice Statistics, there were 765,246 full-time police officers in the United States — roughly 251 police per 100,000 residents.

Below are some of the types of police that serve us:

- **Federal Police:** The federal police officers implement various laws at the federal level as per the authority that is assigned to them under the US Codes.
- **State Police:** They are normally the part of State department of Public Safety. They are operated by the statewide government agencies and the agencies assign duties to them.
- **County Police:** the Sheriff's department provides county law enforcement. The county police mostly exist in the metropolitan

areas. There are three categories of county police such as full service, limited service and restricted service. The full service police provides full spectrum of police services to the entire county. The limited service county police provide services to only the unincorporated areas of the county. And, the restricted service provides security to parks and the various public facilities owned by the county.

- **Municipal Police:** The metropolitan departments have jurisdictions, which cover different municipalities and communities. The municipal police work under these jurisdictions and resolve various jurisdictional problems. They are also appointed on a contract basis to provide full police service to the local cities within the counties.
- **Others:** They are referred to as special purpose police working for various districts. Their functions may vary according to the various jurisdictions. These can be transit police, campus police, airport police, general services police, park police etc.

We all agree that police officers are essential to a modern society. It is hard to think of a role that is more important. We can also agree that no profession is perfect, that every profession has a few folks that are worrisome. We tend to forget that the police are one of the few professions that risk their lives everyday, on our behalf.

There will always be controversy about the role of the police, and there will always be questions about some of the actions that they must take.

Let us ponder the following ideas:

1. Police are essential to our society. No reasonable person can argue otherwise.
2. They risk their lives on our behalf, potentially, everyday.
3. They deserve to be paid well, given the difficult, dangerous, and important jobs they have.
4. We need to stop complaining about the fact that they can retire younger than other professions. Other folks do not have to

chase down criminals when they are in there sixties, on our behalf.

5. Police are often under resourced. Because of a lack of funds training can be woefully inadequate. Training includes knowledge of the law, firearms usage, investigation techniques, crime scene analysis, the list goes on.

6. Would we not be better served by a police force that has the funding to be better trained and better educated?

7. As other professions that are important to society have national certification and training requirements, should not law enforcement have the same?

8. Doesn't it make sense to compensate these folks well, so that we attract the best candidates?

9. Does there need to be some shake-up to do these things? Are some police forces just too small to be resourced and trained properly? Would a police force that covers a much larger area be better resourced, better trained?

10. As other essential professionals are required to carry malpractice insurance, should the need for our law enforcement professionals to carry such policies be discussed or considered?

We may never agree on some issues regarding our police. But let us agree on these things:

1. The **vast majority** of police are people of good character.
2. Their job is tremendously difficult, dangerous, and essential.
3. Many police forces are under resourced. That is on us.
4. And yes, there are some bad apples. But isn't that true of every segment of society? This does not excuse it, but we should at least keep that in mind and not judge all police based on the actions of the very small percentage of "bad cops".
5. Their good work is often not noticed, and is, generally, taken for granted.
6. We need to become more aware as a society of the high cost that police pay for their service.
   Death, injury, PTSD, etc…

17

QUEENS

—

There is a good deal of heated debate about Queens. Not Queen Latifah, everyone loves her, or the rock group, but the kind of Queens that used to rule countries, and are now wealthy figureheads or royalty with limited powers. The debate is actually about monarchy. Should we still have them in the twenty-first century?

Americans seem to be as interested in the British monarchy as the Brits themselves.

Lets examine the British Monarchy:

Monarchy is the oldest form of government in the United Kingdom.

In a monarchy, a king or queen is Head of State. The British Monarchy is known as a constitutional monarchy. This means that, while The Sovereign is Head of State, the ability to make and pass legislation resides with an elected Parliament.

Although The Sovereign no longer has a political or executive role, he or she continues to play an important part in the life of the nation.

As Head of State, The Monarch undertakes constitutional and representational duties, which have developed over one thousand years of history. In addition to these State duties, The Monarch has a less formal role as 'Head of Nation'. The Sovereign acts as a focus for national identity, unity and pride; gives a sense of stability and continuity; officially recognizes success and excellence; and supports the ideal of voluntary service.

In all these roles members of their immediate family support The Sovereign.

The current Queen of Britain is Queen Elizabeth II. She has been queen since 1952. Her son, Prince Charles, heir to the throne, may be wondering if he will ever get a chance to do some kinging.

Americans seem to love the British Royal Family. Little controversy here. Many Americans still admire the late Lady Di, and follow the lives of her two sons Prince Harry and Prince William.

There is a bit of a controversy in the UK as to the appropriateness of a monarchy in a modern world.

Here are some the arguments that are pro monarchy:

1. It creates continuity.
When you are a monarch you are a monarch for life. You are born a future King or Queen. There are no "term limits" thus allowing the Monarch ample time to complete his or her agenda without worrying about elections, or even popularity. Presidents and other members of public office hold their positions for a certain amount of time but the monarch will reign until they die or abdicate. With a permanent presence on the throne, a country can build stable connections with other governments. This has its advantages. With other kinds of governments relationships between countries will differ depending on the view of their head of state.

2. It allows the culture, history and tradition of a nation to be honored and preserved.
A king or queen is a symbol. A symbol that can be rallied behind when the going gets difficult. Supporting the Monarch is a way to demonstrate your patriotism. A constitutional monarch's role isn't just limited to being a symbol. They also serve as a reminder of the culture, history and tradition of their nation.

3. It creates a balance of power.

A monarch may be a non-political head of state but that doesn't mean they shouldn't be asked what to do. Walter Bagehot, a British political theorist, wrote about the three main political rights of a constitutional monarch, which they could freely exercise:

1. The right to be consulted
2. The right to be advised
3. The right to warn.

Yes, a monarch may be limited in power but they also hold critical powers like dissolving parliament, for example.

Monarchs have moral power, and the power of persuasion. They can rally a nation behind important issues.

There are also arguments against monarchy:

1. Monarchs are born into their position.

There are some monarchies where a ruler gets elected but in a constitutional monarchy like the UK's, monarchs are born into their role. They are groomed from birth to be the ruling sovereign of a nation. They get to their position by rules of succession. This makes it rather unfair, as a younger sibling might be a better ruler but the rules of succession make the older one destined for the throne.

2. Achieving progress might be hard.

A government that puts too much weight on traditions and customs is one that will find change slow or difficult. Whether an internal change or any other, a government must make decisions with deference to the monarchy. When this happens, improvements to the system could make progress seem snail paced in a modern world.

3. It is costly.

There are those under a constitutional monarchy who believe that the monarchy is not essential. After all, they have limited powers. But not only is a monarch deemed by critics as unnecessary, they are also extremely expensive to support an extended royal family. The monarch does not pay for the upkeep of their home – the people do that. A lot of people find that unnecessary spending, as monarchs can't benefit their countries because of their limited ruling power.

Certainly monarchies earn money for their nation. Many tourists flock to see the crown jewels, the changing of the guard, etc. Monarchies benefit the economy thru tourism.

The arguments as to monarchy will continue. If we ever have one here, I will vote for Oprah. Nothing against Queen Latifah, she has been a Queen a long time already. If Oprah has too much going on, lets go with Lebron James. Lebron already goes by King James, and he did bring a championship to Cleveland.

18

REPARATIONS

Should there be reparations to African-Americans for slavery?

Here are some Pro reparations arguments:

Reparations should be provided to the descendants of slaves. Reparations are not as unusual concept as many of us believe. American Indians have received reparations from the US government in three ways: 1. Cash Payments 2. Land 3. Tribal Recognition. Germany has been paying substantial reparations to Israel since 1953 for slave labor and the holocaust. They negotiated to pay Israel to what amounts to $13,600,000,000 if the Native Americans and Jews deserve reparations (is that seriously in doubt?) certainly so do African Americans.

Free labor provided by slavery accounted for a great deal of the wealth of this country, and much of the western world. When you start talking about "old money" in our country you are talking about wealth brought about from slave labor. Many major corporations still in existence today profited greatly from slavery. This wealth which, was built on the backs of slaves, should be shared with the descendants of those slaves. This is not an unusual legal concept.

After the emancipation of slaves African Americans faced a century of open legal and social oppression at the hand of their former slave masters (From 1860-1960.) Much of it codified in the law. After the tokenist measures passed in the 1960's African Americans still have not seen any real change in their socioeconomic status. Over half of the prison population in the U.S is African American while they only account for 17% of the population. Over half of African Americans live below the federal poverty line.

Unemployment rates for African Americans stays consistently in the 20's; while federal unemployment rates almost never rise above 15. The fact is

African Americans still suffer from the open oppression of their former slave masters and their children.

WEB Dubois said in The Souls of Black Folk, " (The African American) He felt his poverty; without a cent, without a home, without land, tools, or savings, he had entered into competition with rich, landed, skilled neighbors. To be a poor man is hard, but to be a poor race in a land of dollars is the very bottom of hardships. He felt the weight of his ignorance- not simply of letters, but of life, of business, of the humanities; the accumulated sloth and shirking and awkwardness of decades and centuries shackled his hands and feet. Nor was his burden all poverty and ignorance. The red stain of bastardry, which two centuries of systematic legal defilement of Negro women had stamped upon his race, meant not only the loss of ancient African chastity, but also the hereditary weight of a mass of corruption from white adulterers, threatening almost the obliteration of the Negro home. A people thus handicapped ought not to be asked to race with the world" without reparations.

Arguments against reparations:

Reparations serve no purpose in the modern United States they are based on the idea the Black People are owed financial aide from people who never oppressed them. The US government already assists people of all races.

Here is what the government is already doing:

High unemployment rate among black people? Unemployment Benefits and Job Fares.

High hunger rate among black people? Food Stamps.

High poverty rate among black people? Negative Tax Rates.

Low Education rate among black people? Pell Grants.

Almost every issue facing blacks has a pre-existing program (both federal and charitable) meant to help. Reparations serve no role in fixing these issues, but leads to numerous problems, such as calculating the amount of blame per person.

Japanese-Americans were compensated for being sent to internment camps during World War II. The compensation was too little too late. To our credit, at least it was done. These were American citizens that were basically locked up because of their country of origin. This did not happen to Americans of German or Italian descent, folks that also had heritages with nations we were at war with. It should be pointed out that many of these Japanese-American men that were interred volunteered to fight for the United States during World War II in the European Theatre. Their unit suffered extremely high casualty rates and was among the most decorated units in US military history.

19

SPACE EXPLORATION

—

Somewhat surprisingly space exploration is controversial. To be specific, the *cost* of space exploration is hotly debated (except among Star Trek fans).

Wouldn't this money be better spent on earth? Why don't we take that money and use it to research a cure for cancer? Why not become the best species we can be, and reach for the stars?

There are some significant points in favor of space research and exploration.

1. Space research and exploration has an excellent track record of bringing changes to our everyday lives by introducing **breakthroughs in scientific knowledge** and opening doors to new information that might otherwise have been undiscovered. In fact, space exploration has already benefited us in numerous ways. Satellites help locate minerals and fossil fuels. We have been able to harness solar energy due to our knowledge of the sun, something that will become increasingly important as we deal with greenhouse gases and their effects. . Scientists are trying to understand if the process by which heat and light energy is produced by the sun, can be replicated on Earth to generate energy for human use. Through space exploration, we may be able to find new energy sources. This field paves the path for the study of cosmic radiations and their effects and uses.

2. Space exploration can help us gain knowledge of other planets, stars, solar systems and other celestial bodies. It has the potential to resolve some of the many mysteries of outer space. Other life forms may be discovered through space exploration. We may discover completely different life forms on another planet that supports life. Or we might find a planet that can sustain life. Perhaps one day it could be colonized. We may even find new human-like species, or aliens who are more developed than us. Exploring space may lead us to the discovery of an all-new world, and new species.

3. Our knowledge of the earth has increased due to space exploration. Scientists are able to study the Earth's atmosphere from space and understand the changes in climate and their effects on the life on Earth. Because of space travel it is possible to observe our planet from a distance. Satellites help science assess how well and for how long our planet will be able to sustain life. Changes in the environment, and issues like climate change and ozone depletion are studied. Space exploration has helped answer questions like how the Earth was formed or where organic materials come from.

4. The space program is a job creator, especially for scientists. Government agencies such as NASA have thousands of employees. Space programs create significant employment. Space exploration involves astronomy, physics, and space technology. These fields create work opportunities for not just astronauts, but even scientists and engineers who work on unmanned spacecraft, astronomers who study objects in space, and professionals who work in designing and testing space equipment. The skills they hone can be transferred to other areas.

5. The space program provides our species some self-defense.

By exploring space, scientists know when an asteroid is going to pass close to Earth orbit or whether there are chances of it striking our planet and the potential harm it may cause. Asteroids that may threaten life on Earth can be mapped, thanks to space research. Scientists have even been able to devise ways to prevent the impact of asteroids by diverting objects approaching us.

6. Space research requires the use of advanced state of the art technology, including specialized communication devices, computers, robots, and other equipment. Space exploration has a proven potential to drive scientific innovation.

7. Space exploration encourages the human desire for adventure and progress. Those willing to risk their lives life for the space program earn the relevant education and work with a space research orga-

nization. They participate in space studies and some of them even have the opportunity to travel to space. Space exploration satisfies the human need to achieve great things.

8. Space programs lead to a high level of cooperation between nations. Different nations come together in the pursuit of a common goal. When space research agencies come together, resources and expenses are shared and the research costs do not burden a single country. This may lay the groundwork for other areas of cooperation. Space studies bring researchers from different parts of the world together, thus achieving a sharing of knowledge and setting a tone of co-operative effort.

There are also arguments against space programs:

1. Manned missions pose a great risk, perhaps an unacceptable risk to the astronauts. Space exploration risks human life. Space travel is not easy; the conditions are harsh, making survival during space travel a challenge. Effects of radiation on the body and bone loss resulting from microgravity are some of the significant health related issues that arise from space travel. Unmanned missions eliminate these dangers, but as robots have to be utilized, additional technology costs are incurred.

2. The most important argument against space exploration is the amount of money that is spent. Space travel is extraordinarily costly. The research undertaken needs the implementation of advanced technology, further adding to the costs. Because of the time that needs to be invested compared to the outcome, the research may not prove to be cost-effective. The cost of education for this field is also very high. The money that is spent on space exploration can be spent to reduce poverty and a host of other things. A nations wealth can be directed to other things that may help people in immediate need. A huge amount of money is required for traveling to space. Critics of space exploration argue that it is not right to spend money on something

like space research when millions of people on the planet are unable to meet even their most basic needs.

3. The exploration of space could bring us existential trouble. In space, we may find something that is lethal to the life on Earth and bring it back.

4. Cooperation among nations may be cited as an advantage of space exploration. It may actually lead to disputes between and within nations. Satellites could be used by one country to spy on another. Even attack another. Among arguments against space travel is that it may be conducted with the wrong intentions. This may lead to strained relations between countries and an unhealthy competition.

5. Space junk, or debris, is accumulating at alarming rates and is too expensive to clean up with current technologies. This space junk impacts further space
Exploration and can fall to earth.

6. Space exploration can mean a "major leap for mankind." However, it is also criticized by some for not having achieved many major scientific breakthroughs. Public interest can serve as the determinant in judging the suitability of space exploration. It may not be wise to make such huge expenses on space exploration if other human needs are being ignored or left unfulfilled. But the hope to find extraterrestrial life thrives on space exploration.
To many space exploration is the final frontier, something we must pursue. To others, it represents an immoral use of resources that could be spent on human needs. Can we strike a delicate balance? Perhaps not. But there are certainly good people on both sides of this debate. Pro space exploration people are not against helping the unfortunate here on planet earth. Anti-space exploration folks are not anti-science.

20

TESTING

———

Testing, testing, and more testing. Elementary school through high school we are doing more and more of it. More time testing equals less time teaching students, there is, after all, a finite amount of time teachers have with their students. How much testing is too much testing? Is too much of a good thing bad? Professional educators, parents, and politicians debate the amount of testing seriously. It is often stated that schools (teachers) " must be held accountable". True, but is this the best way to do it? Aren't students and parents stakeholders in the educational process too?

What does testing actually tell us?

It's not difficult at all to find a professional educator willing to talk with you at length about the amount of standardized testing in our schools today, and the pressures for test preparation. How common are these concerns among teachers? How does this actually impact the teaching of our children?

New data suggests the notion of over-testing and test preparation is more than just anecdotal concerns: They are the reality for most of our public-school teachers.

Eighty-one percent of educators are of the opinion that their students spend far too much time taking tests mandated by their state or local school district, according to research by the Center on Educational Study based out of The George Washington University.

How much time is too much? On average, students spend about **ten** days taking district-mandated tests during the school year and **nine** days taking state-mandated tests, teachers estimate. But underneath these averages are wide variations, from less than a week to more than a month, the research finds.

When it comes to test preparation, approximately 62 percent of teachers say they spend too much time getting their students ready for the state-mandated exams. To be clear, they are required to do so. Also, 51 percent feel the same way about district-required tests, according to the nationally representative survey conducted in late 2015.

Not all test prep is the same. It can mean many different things, some good, some not so. The CEP report defines it as "drilling students on specific content and skills covered on the tests, using practice tests, and/or teaching test-taking skills like time-management and pacing."

Test prep is especially prevalent in high-poverty and medium-poverty schools, according to the survey. Thirty-six percent of teachers spend at least a month on test prep for state-mandated exams, for example. By contrast, the figure is 23 percent in low-poverty schools. A lot of time is spent on test prep.

These are just some of the findings from the Center on Education Policy report (completed with financial support of the Bill & Melinda Gates Foundation). It's based on a survey of more than 3,000 teachers. The data, issued recently, offers fresh insights into the views of classroom teachers on testing, standards, the Common Core implementation and other issues.

There has been a good deal of research of late on teacher morale. Much of it strongly indicates that many teachers are losing a commitment to their field amid multiple and varied frustrations, including pressures around testing.

"While the teaching profession in the United States may not be in full blown crisis, forces outside of teachers' control may be taxing their good will and dedication," the report says. "The most important stressors indicated by the current research are the time devoted to testing, changing demands from outside the classroom, and teachers' perceptions that they lack a voice in major decisions."

Maria Ferguson, the Center on Education Policy's executive director, offered a preview of some of the research findings during a seminar titled "Teaching and Testing in the Common Core Era."

Among the challenges she cited for teachers was the "constantly changing slate of demands on teachers." Ferguson said it's worth further exploring the extent to which such circumstances impede effective teaching.

Certainly, recent changes in state testing systems have been a major adjustment for educators. Many states that had planned to use Common Core assessments developed by two major testing consortia have recently shifted gears and gone their own way.

Whatever assessments teachers encounter, the CEP data indicate that the time spent on testing is too much for most teachers. Only 16 percent report that time for state- and district-mandated tests was about right, and a microscopic1 percent say it is not enough.

The amount of time teachers reported for such assessments varies widely.

As we have seen earlier in this book, this nation has far fewer days in a school year than many believe necessary. Are too many of these days spent testing as opposed to teaching? Is there a true benefit to children to the amount of testing completed?

A cattle farmer once said " a cow ain't gonna gain weight just cause you keep weighing it. " Maybe he was on to something there.

Politicians and school boards gain some credibility by demanding more testing. Are we doing too much testing? Does this testing have real benefit? It appears as though it is here to stay.

21

UNIONS

—

People should have a say in their lives. They should not be taken advantage of unfairly by those with more power. They should be free to join together to address those in authority. Are we talking about freedom? Democracy? Yes. But we are also talking about unions.

Unions. A topic of emotional debate to be sure.

When discussing the pros and cons of unions, it is important to remember that unions have helped all of us, whether or not we have ever been a union member.

1. Unions Gave Us The Weekend: Even the conservative Mises Institute notes that the relatively labor-free 1870, the average workweek for most Americans was 61 hours—almost double what most Americans work now. In the late nineteenth century and the twentieth century, labor unions engaged in huge strikes in order to demand shorter workweeks so that Americans could be home with their loved ones instead of constantly working for their employers with no leisure time. Talk about family values! By 1937, these labor actions created political momentum to pass the Fair Labor Standards Act, which helped create a federal framework for a shorter workweek that included room for leisure time.

2. Unions Gave Us Fair Wages And Relative Income Equality: As Think-Progress has reported the relative decline of unions over the past 35 years closely mirrored a decline in the middle class's share of the national income. It is also true that at the time when most Americans belonged to a union between the 1940's and 1950's—income inequality in the U.S. was at its lowest point in the history of our country.

3. Unions Helped End Child Labor: "Union organizing and child labor reform were often intertwined" in American history, with organization's like the "National Consumers' League" and the National Child Labor Committee" working together in the early 20th century to ban child labor. The very first American Federation of Labor (AFL) national convention passed "a resolution calling on states to ban all children under 14 from all gainful employment" in 1881, and soon after states across the country adopted similar recommendations, leading up to the 1938 Fair Labor Standards Act which regulated child labor on the federal level for the very first time.

4. Unions Won Widespread Employer-Based Health Coverage: "The rise of unions in the 1930's and 1940's led to the first great expansion of health care" for all Americans, as labor unions banded workers together to negotiate for health coverage plans from employers. In 1942, "the US set up a National War Labor Board. It had the power to set a cap on all wage increases. But it let employers circumvent the cap by offering "fringe benefits"—notably, health insurance." By 1950, "half of all companies with fewer than 250 workers and 2/3 of all companies with more than 250 workers offered health insurance of one kind or another."

5. Unions Spearheaded The Fight For The Family And Medical Leave Act: Labor unions like the AFL-CIO federation led the fight for this 1993 law, which "require state agencies and private employers with more than 50 employees to provide up to 12 weeks of job-protected unpaid leave annually for workers to care for a newborn, newly adopted child, seriously ill family member or for the worker's own illness."

There are certainly pros and cons to unions:

Pro: Unions have the power to negotiate higher wages, improved benefits and better working conditions for their members. This ensures adequate compensation, fair coverage and increased safety for union workers.

Con: Union negotiations can lead to wages and other associated costs being boosted to unreasonably high levels. If a company is not able to sustain the high wages and costs for union workers, then it is left with several options. It can raise prices on the goods or services it provides. It can outsource its labor, perhaps send it overseas. It can reduce the number of new hire employees, leaving an insufficient workforce to manage the overall workload. None of these options are desirable to employees, and they can lead to a potentially difficult workplace environment.

Another issue is labor union dues and fees. In some cases, dues and fees offset the higher, union-negotiated wages.

Job Protection and Job Security

Pro: Unionized employees are guaranteed union advocacy in the workplace. The union, not the employer, has the power to determine disciplinary actions, including termination, which generally equates to greater job security.

Con: Union protection makes it difficult for employers to discipline, terminate or even promote employees. There is also a cronyism aspect to unions. Unions can decide whom they accept into their group. Therefore, membership in many unions becomes less about skill and competency and more about networking or "clout".

Balance of Power

Pro: A union gives workers power through a collective voice. Employers have no choice but to negotiate with unions in order to maintain productivity. The right to strike is the ultimate show of worker empowerment

Con: The necessary tension between employers and employees resulting from labor unions is often counterproductive. The combative nature of the relationship promotes workplace hostility rather than workplace cooperation and collaboration. A contentious environment may be the result.

Unlike non-union workers, unionized employees are bound to follow majority rule regarding strikes. This leads to loss of income for the employees and loss of profit for the company. Additionally, striking does not often garner public approval. If labor union workers already earn more than non-union workers, striking makes them seem self-serving.

The pros and cons of labor unions are largely a matter of position and perception. Unions do offer distinct advantages to employees, but decreasing membership suggests that those advantages may no longer be enough in the modern workplace. From an overall perspective, the most apparent benefits may be offset by corresponding disadvantages. That being said let's recognize:

1. Unions have done a lot of good for society, for members and non-members alike.
2. Union members often make more money than their non-union counterparts. Rather than focusing on the union members making more, shouldn't there be a focus on non-union workers being paid better, especially in industries where the CEO's are making tens of millions of dollars a year?
3. Though unions do have negatives, isn't it necessary for workers to have some protections?
4. Unions are often involved in making sure their members are competent and well trained. All things considered, would you want your brakes repaired by a union worker whose union mandates a high level of training or non-union worker who is going to complete the job at a cheaper price?

Again, we may have to agree to disagree about unions.

22

VETERANS AFFAIRS PRIVATIZATION

—

Most of us think the VA is the Veterans Administration. It is now the Department of Veterans Affairs. We all support the Vets, but there is considerable debate as to whether or not the Veterans Hospitals should be privatized. Lets first take a look at what the VA hospitals actually are.

The hospital system of the Department of Veterans Affairs (VA), formerly the Veterans Administration, represents the principal way the government provides medical care directly to civilians. It does so in close collaboration with the nation's medical schools, providing a major resource for educating physicians and other health care workers. This educational mission has grown in importance as medical school faculty members turn increasingly to the practice of medicine to earn the money they need to survive and as the Health Care Financing Administration loses enthusiasm for including the cost of medical education in its funding of health care.

During the last decade, the budget for health care in community hospitals has escalated by about 10 percent a year, in spite of aggressive attempts to limit its growth. During the same period, the $11 billion budget of the VA hospital system has increased only 2 percent a year, while maintaining a relatively steady workload and satisfactory quality.

In 1989 serious financial limitations forced the government for the first time to reduce the VA's workload by about 10 percent through limits on the number of veterans eligible for care. This change has created underused capacity that could be made available for other purposes or kept as a strategic reserve for the future demands of an aging population of veterans. Government.

Political, educational, and economic situations dictate that a separate medical system for veterans will continue to exist unless the present varied structure is replaced by some sort of centralized national program. It seems important that the federal government to recognize the VA hospital system as a national asset and to use it to study ways to improve the efficiency of providing medical services.

Approximately 30,000,000 Americans are veterans of military service and thus potentially eligible for VA care. Until the 1980s, eligibility requirements were lax. Basically, any veteran could receive care in VA facilities, although those with disabilities associated with military service ("service connected") had priority. Most veterans, however, did not use the VA system, and most of the 15 percent who did come to VA hospitals had service-connected disabilities or were very poor.

Given this trend, and in response to a decreasing budget for the VA system, Congress recently redefined the rules of eligibility. Only those who have service-connected disabilities or whose income falls below a poverty line set at about $18,000 per couple became eligible for treatment in VA hospitals. This tightening of eligibility requirements resulted in a decrease of about 10 percent in hospital admissions, and it has given the VA system fiscal viability in 1990.

Although the United States had not been involved in a major war since 1973, there will be a large number of veterans through at least the first quarter of the 21st century. . The increasing age of veterans, 95 percent of whom are men, will expand their need for medical services even as their total number gradually declines. Recognizing the projected graying of its clientele, the VA has taken a national role of leadership in geriatric research and care.

Aging veterans are, of course, increasingly eligible for health coverage under Medicare. Why do patients who are entitled to Medicare or Medicaid coverage continue to come to VA facilities? For poor people, totally free medical care is preferable to care involving the 20 percent copayment required by Medicare (which may increase in the future). Patients who choose the VA tend to like it and view the local VA hospital as their own. Loyal and appreciative patients attract loyal staff members who stay as long as the conditions of employment are reasonable.

The VA's 171 hospitals are scattered about the country as historical precedent, political influence, demographic need, and educational pressure have dictated. The mission of these hospitals varies from full-fledged tertiary care to long-term psychiatric care or rehabilitation, and their facilities vary from those of academic institutions to those of small community hospitals or nursing homes. In addition, the VA operates a number of freestanding clinics that provide ambulatory care. Most of the VA's facilities are old, and the physical plants are relatively inefficient, but the department continued to build new facilities in the 1970s (in San Antonio, Lexington, Ky., and San Diego, for example) and 1980s (in Portland, Oregon, Seattle, Minneapolis, and Baltimore, for example). The uncertainties of federal funding and fierce political pressure have precluded a systematic program of hospital modernization, replacement, or relocation. In the past, the pressures of reduced budgets and fewer patients in acute care hospitals have resulted in the consolidation of neighboring hospitals and the reassignment of responsibilities. In 1989, for example, the VA hospital in Newington, Connecticut, transferred its surgical and short-term psychiatric services to the West Haven, Connecticut, hospital but expanded its programs in geriatric and long-term psychiatric care. The resulting realignment of responsibilities has improved the efficiency of both hospitals. Further realignments will be needed before the system achieves its most effective configuration.

Before World War II, the VA's program of medical care was an isolated "warehousing" system that cared for a few veterans of World War I. It was operated by the Civil Service Commission in hospitals far from centers of population and largely divorced from the mainstream of contemporary medical practice. When World War II ended in 1945, this program was incapable of providing appropriate care to the young veterans in military hospitals.

General Omar Bradley was appointed administrator of the VA, and his mission was to remedy this situation. Realizing that the VA was responsible for 100,000 hospitalized veterans and that the postwar shortage of physicians made it impossible to hire enough doctors, Dr. Paul Magnuson, Bradley's chief medical officer, proposed inviting medical schools to affiliate with VA hospitals. The schools — financially depleted by the wartime acceleration of the medical curriculum and under great pressure to complete the education of young physicians whose careers had been interrupted by military service — welcomed the opportunity.

Dr. Magnuson's proposal committed the VA to operating the hospitals, while giving the medical schools full control of education and the recruitment of physicians. General Bradley persuaded Congress to implement the program by creating the VA Department of Medicine and Surgery, free from the restrictions of the Civil Service Commission. The affiliation program has continued to function under a simple policy statement that makes the VA responsible for operating the affiliated hospitals and the medical schools responsible for recruiting medical staff, carrying out the educational program, and maintaining the quality of medical care. Many such relationships were quickly established, and soon 133 (of 171) VA hospitals are affiliated with 102 medical schools as dean's-committee hospitals. The hospitals that are not affiliated are generally isolated units that account for only a small percentage of the VA's patients and expenditures.

The early VA hospitals were mixtures of acute care facilities, rehabilitation centers, nursing homes, and domiciliary homes for indigent veterans. Gradually, the length of stay has become shorter and the use of hospital beds solely for the convenience of the patients had ceased. In the early years, ambulatory care was forbidden, but the need for evaluation before admission, preventive medicine, and follow-up after discharge resulted in the development of a system of clinics. In 1972 Congress required that ambulatory care be made available, and since the late 1980s the VA has been a comprehensive health care system. The system provides medications and essential social services prescribed by VA physicians. The pattern of diseases treated by the VA has also changed: the number of patients with tuberculosis has decreased enormously, and ambulatory programs have been developed for patients with chronic psychiatric disorders. The VA is increasingly concerned with treating acute episodes of disease in patients with all types of chronic conditions, including the disorders of the elderly and severe psychiatric disabilities.

The VA is much different today.

The role of the VA in health education has grown steadily since the inception of dean's-committee affiliations in 1946. In the late 1960s the movement to increase the number of physicians led to the establishment of new medical schools, some of which based their entire clinical program in a VA-affiliated hospital. For example, in its early days the program of Louisiana State University at Shreveport was entirely encompassed by its VA hospital. Other schools increased the size of their classes during the 1960s and became increasingly dependent on the VA for adequate opportunities for clinical teaching the same trend has occurred in the education of other health care professionals. Currently, more than 1000 professional schools are affiliated with VA hospitals, and every year more than 100,000 students in health care disciplines receive all or part of their clinical experience in VA facilities. Since about a third of all medical students spend some time in VA medical centers during each of their years of clinical training, most medical students have considerable educational experience in VA hospitals.

Moreover, every year about 40 percent of the nation's house officers rotate through a VA facility. By the end of their medical training, most American physicians have had substantial exposure to VA medicine.

The degree to which medical schools depend on their VA teaching hospitals varies with location. The newer schools tend to be more dependent than the older schools on the VA's educational resources. The true needs of medical schools for access to the VA system can be estimated from the amount of time medical students and house staff spend in their affiliated VA hospitals. In most major affiliated VA facilities, the training programs are fully integrated with the medical school's program, and a single appointment embraces both residencies.

At the University of California at San Diego, for example, both medical students and medical house officers spend 50 percent or more of their time in the VA hospital. Many other medical schools would find it difficult to fulfill their clinical-teaching responsibilities without a VA affiliation.

The educational value of the VA's facilities is increasing, even in places where the hospitals had once seemed somewhat redundant. In university and community hospitals, many patients are admitted only after an initial workup has been completed by their private physician or in an outpatient clinic, and patients are discharged shortly after the completion of the diagnostic or therapeutic maneuver that prompted their admission. Obviously, this pattern of care is relatively unsuitable to the education of medical students and house staff.

In contrast, the VA deals mostly with patients who attend its clinics, and valid social or physical reasons often lead to more prolonged inpatient care. The VA thus provides an educational opportunity in continuity of care that is increasingly difficult to duplicate in other hospital settings. Because the faculty at VA medical centers is identical to that of the affiliated medical school, this education can be carried out without sacrificing quality, provided that the VA facility is comparable in efficiency and resources to a medical school hospital.

In 1973 the National Academy of Sciences established a commission, chaired by Dr. Saul Farber, to evaluate the role of the VA system. The commission's report described a number of important problems, including constructing new facilities in places where there were already too many hospital beds while failing to provide for other (especially rural) areas that lacked adequate facilities. It criticized the VA for accepting patients whose disabilities were not service connected and who had the resources to obtain care in underused community facilities and for tolerating functional inefficiencies that were unacceptable in community hospitals. The commission paid tribute, however, to the important role of the VA in caring for patients with spinal-cord injuries and chronic psychiatric disease, and recognized that its clientele chose the VA, "where they are treated with dignity. In general they are satisfied with their treatment and with the availability of the VA medical care."

In discussing these findings, Relman characterized the VA system as a "sacred cow" whose "redundancies and inefficiencies should not be ignored. Both the Farber Commission and Relman recommended integrating the VA system into the national civilian health care program, probably through the institution of universal health care insurance. Ginzberg considered this suggestion politically unrealistic, since universal health insurance was not likely to be instituted.

The VA responded by acknowledging some of the system's defects. Many of the criticisms contained in the Farber report have since been addressed, and the success of this effort is reflected in the VA system today Fiscal incentives helped shorten the periods of hospitalization, but attempts to close some inefficient hospitals led to such political bloodshed that the closure of hospitals has disappeared from the VA's lexicon. Reform was undoubtedly speeded by the Reagan administration's belief in removing government from nonessential operations, a belief that threatened to transfer the VA to the private sector. Meanwhile, changes in the private-hospital system have produced a shortage of beds in many areas, and the excess of beds that worried the Farber Commission is no longer important in most places. Political opposition and the recognition of some of the VA's special functions have eliminated the threat of transferring the system to the private sector to many. However, the policy of reducing the VA's budget while maintaining its assigned workload has presented the central administration of the VA with a serious challenge. In response, it has modified the system of diagnosis-related groups to create a method for allocating resources within the department, and it has established an aggressive program to review the quality of medical care.

The improving efficiency generated by the VA's current leadership has provided a sound and realistic fiscal defense of the present system, although it is recognized that certain problems remain. These include a continued degree of redundancy, noncompetitive salary levels, and the need to upgrade the physical plant and equipment of some VA hospitals.

Unfortunately, the VA's methods of evaluating clinical costs are not correlated with those used by the Health Care Financing Administration, so direct comparisons between the agencies cannot be made. This is regrettable at a time when the government needs to look carefully at the costs and possible advantages of providing comprehensive rather than fee-for-service care. In 1985 John Iglehart, the *Journal's* national correspondent, wrote a two-part article_about the VA system and its future. He came to the tentative conclusion that the VA was less costly than the private sector, in part because the Reagan administration was reported to have seriously considered replacing the VA system with medical vouchers to be used in the private sector, but found the idea far too expensive to pursue. This conclusion is especially impressive when one considers that the VA system's costs include the salaries of physicians and other health care specialists, which are excluded from hospital costs in the calculations of the Health Care Financing Administration.

Fiscal and Workload Data from the San Diego VA Medical Center. which sets forth the workload of the VA medical center in San Diego over the past few years, is instructive and illustrative. The hospital budget increased less than two percent a year, whereas measures of workload — the number of admissions and the number of patients requiring medical intensive care — increased by 2.6 and 7.0 percent, respectively. This trend, which is reported by many of our colleagues throughout the VA system, has led to serious problems in maintaining the quality of care and staff. In the face of these difficulties, how well has the VA maintained medical standards? Evaluating the quality of medical care is difficult, especially when comparing patients in private-sector hospitals with indigent, often malnourished VA patients who lack social-support systems and who have a high incidence of addiction to tobacco, alcohol, and drugs. These factors contribute to the longer average length of stay in VA hospitals than in community hospitals. Nonetheless, it is remarkable that in all national measurements of medical quality the VA remains well within the middle third of the rankings.

Since 1946 the VA has supported a productive research effort that has achieved a worldwide reputation for excellence, and two VA investigators have won Nobel prizes. Originally, VA research served two objectives — expanding the frontiers of knowledge and providing a tool for the recruitment and training of physicians in the VA system. Although the first objective has continued to be of primary importance, the second has suffered as competition for VA funding has become almost as fierce as that for funding from the National Institutes of Health. Between 1980 and the VA's fiscal nadir in 1988, the budget for biomedical research rose only from $115 million to $159 million, but this increment represented a decline from about 2 to about 1.6 percent of the VA's hospital care budget, a reduction of 20 percent. Only about 70 percent of the budget of the Medical Research Service goes directly to biomedical research, the remainder being used for cooperative studies, career-development awards, and administrative expenses. Thus, only 1.1 percent of the total VA medical budget is devoted to biomedical research. In constant dollars, the funds allocated to medical research have fallen from $148 million in 1984 to $140 million in 1990, a drop of more than 5 percent. This substantial reduction has impaired the VA's ability to compete for the best young physicians.

The Cooperative Studies Program has been especially valuable because it allows access to large numbers of patients for enrollment in sophisticated clinical trials. The VA is the paramount resource for evaluating such problems as the effectiveness of estrogens in the treatment of prostatic cancer, the value of coronary bypass surgery, the best chemotherapy for tuberculosis, the optimal pharmacologic treatment of epilepsy, and the efficacy of controlling hypertension in preventing strokes. The VA's facilities for conducting these trials include special centers for statistical support and an experimental pharmacy.

It should be recognized, however, that in spite of its success in studying the clinical usefulness of some treatments, the VA system has been underused in evaluations of the cost or effectiveness of many other methods of patient care. For example, although it cares for a large number of patients with chronic respiratory disease, the VA has many fewer respiratory therapists than community hospitals. The VA's therapeutic results appear, however, to be at least as good. If a properly conducted study of efficacy and costs showed that the VA's staffing pattern was adequate, other hospitals could probably save millions in this area alone. Such studies might easily be designed to compare the patterns of practice in a VA hospital with those in its medical school counterpart. Within such an educational complex, differences in patterns of medical practice are more likely to reflect differences in economic or social motivation than differences in philosophy. Other treatments whose costs and efficacy might be compared include coronary-artery bypass grafting, prostatectomy, herniorrhaphy, and noncurative radiation therapy.

Another issue in urgent need of study is the cost effectiveness of treatment for borderline hypercholesterolemia. Controlling cholesterol is an important therapeutic and cost—benefit question, because the VA provides care to a population of elderly men with coronary heart disease, diabetes, peripheral vascular disease, and strokes. Other than dietary intervention, however, the available treatments (especially the drugs, such as lovastatin, that inhibit 3-hydroxy-3-methylglutaryl-coenzyme A reductase activity) are quite expensive.[14] Twenty percent of the approximately 30,000 patients at the San Diego VA Medical Center have serum cholesterol levels of 6.2 mmol per liter (240 mg per deciliter) or higher and should, according to the expert panel of the National Institutes of Health, receive therapy.[15] Their treatment with lovastatin would cost $2 million each year, adding 3 to 4 percent to the medical center's budget. If our figures can be extrapolated, such drug therapy for hypercholesterolemia might add $10 billion to $20 billion a year to the national health care budget. We urgently need to know whether this is the best way to spend so much money.

There is another area — the study of health care administration — in which the VA should be a leader but in which it is ineffective. One of every three dollars spent on health care in the United States is a government dollar. This represents a total government expense of more than $200 billion annually, an amount that will surely increase, as will the percentage of the gross national product spent on health care. Responsible government should be devising ways to look at the cost—benefit effects of interventions in patient care. The Health Care Financing Administration is undertaking a major program to evaluate and improve medical practice by monitoring the patterns of practice in the Medicare and Medicaid population that it finances.18 It appears, however, to have completely ignored a population of perhaps 2 million patients eligible for Medicare but in fact cared for by the VA. The reporting and research systems of the Health Care Financing Administration and the VA are different, and they would have to be standardized to permit comparisons, but such comparisons could be especially useful as new proposals for a national system of health care are made.

Above is a summary of the important part the VA medical care system plays in the education of medical professionals in the United States, its notable contribution to biomedical and clinical research, and its proved ability to provide medical care to indigent and eligible veterans. I have also noted that the VA's efficiency could be improved by modifying the distribution of resources, adjusting the mission of its facilities to reflect changing needs, and providing better continuity of care, especially for the aging population of veterans. One should recognize the urgent need to limit the fiscal burden of the current U.S. system of fee-for-service medical care, and we suggest ways in which the VA system — as a national health service — could be used as a model for comparison with the mainstream medical establishment, including Medicare and Medicaid. Our recommendations for pursuing these considerations are summarized in the following paragraphs.

First, the VA should continue to examine the justification for the 171 medical centers it now operates. The mission of some facilities is already changing to accommodate new needs associated with changes in the VA's patient population. Such reexamination and reconfiguration should be encouraged. The end result should be a more efficient system, with redundancies removed and resources allocated where need exists, especially for the growing group of aging veterans who will need improved medical and social support.

Second, to minimize the need to institutionalize aging veterans, the VA must improve the continuity of medical care. An important component should be streamlined ambulatory services similar to those available in the private sector. The characteristics of these new ambulatory services should include prompt response time, the elimination of long waits for appointments or admission to medical care, assignment of a specific physician to provide each patient with continuity of care, and integration of inpatient and ambulatory medical care. Such changes would greatly enhance the value of the VA in medical education.

Third, because the VA has recently restricted the use of its facilities to indigent patients or those whose illnesses are related to military service, VA facilities are now somewhat underused at a time of inadequate health care for the indigent. This suggests two important new functions for the VA system.

As a first, experimental step, the eligibility of veterans with service-connected disabilities and indigent veterans with disabilities that are not service connected could be extended to their dependents. This would permit comparison of the advantages and disadvantages of a federal health facility — essentially a national health service — competing with the present system of Medicare and Medicaid insurance. The experiment would be limited enough to be reversible, if that proved advisable, but extensive enough to give solid information. Since this change would transfer patients from Medicare and Medicaid, Congress might have to reassign funds, but as a first step, the modification could be restricted to a few areas where the need for reallocation was minimal. In any case, the experiment would require only the reallocation of funds already earmarked for clinical care, rather than an increase in the current level of federal health funding.

If this experiment were successful, it might justify expanding VA eligibility to include a wider population of indigent nonveterans. Such a change would represent a major political decision, which would only be justified if the physical plant and the quality of VA medical care were comparable to those of the community.

Finally, the potential value of the VA system for research into health care delivery systems should be expanded through focused evaluations of the cost effectiveness and efficacy of newly developed treatments undertaken before they become entrenched in medical practice without adequate scientific justification. Such a step will require an increase in the research funding allocated to cooperative studies and health care delivery in the VA, since it would be damaging to cut further the present level of funding for basic and clinical research. It will also probably require that the VA's methods of evaluating performance (for example, the system of diagnosis-related groups) be made comparable with those of the Health Care Financing Administration and third-party insurance carriers.

The VA health care system is a valuable asset. It is necessary to our present level of medical education. It can provide a laboratory for studying the efficiency and effectiveness of clinical and administrative techniques, and it can be used to clarify some of the issues involved in providing all Americans with high-quality medical care at an affordable price.

When it comes to the pros of veteran health care privatization, there are a few potential positive elements to it. Some examples include easier access to care and potential cost savings. This section is going to cover some of these items in greater detail.

Here are some of the "pros" to VA hospital privatization:

1.Cost Savings Potential

One <u>positive element of the privatization</u> of veteran healthcare that is frequently cited is its potential cost savings. Privatization would allow veterans to choose from a wider range of private health care professionals. Many of these have lower fees than other options available. The ability to shop for a more affordable care provider would then result in potential cost savings.

2. Wait Time Reduction

One of the biggest issues plaguing the current veteran health care system is its long waits for even the most standard care. This is where privatization would shine the most when it comes to improving veteran care.

With a private system, veterans could pick from a wide variety of in-network physicians that are approved based on their given plan. This way, they could receive access to the care they need in a fast and efficient manner. This would include access to a specialist when needed as well.

The reduction in wait times also has the potential to help decrease costs further. It does this by helping to ensure veterans are treated before their conditions worsen. By treating conditions as they arise, we can appropriately handle them before they evolve into more complicated ailments that require more invasive treatment options.

3. Location Availability

Another issue with the current veteran health care system is the location of approved VA hospitals. For many veterans, this results in lengthy travel times to reach there nearest approved hospital. This results in a further delay in treatment and is a major inconvenience to our veterans.

With a privatized system, the network of approved physicians and hospitals would be greatly expanded. This helps to increase the likelihood that veterans will find an office location that is close and convenient for them.

The Cons Of Veteran Health care Privatization

While there are several benefits to privatizing veteran healthcare, there are also several drawbacks as well. This section is going to cover several of those elements like loss of specialization, the potential for higher costs, and more. Continue reading to discover some of the potential cons of veteran health care privatization.

1. Potential Increase In Costs

While it is true that some studies state that privatization can possibly reduce operating costs, there are also studies that show that privatization would actually increase the costs associated with veteran care. This is due to key differences in <u>how the current system and a private one would operate</u>.

In the current system, the government pays for all veteran health care centers and all workers are given a set salary. Their payments do not change based on factors like surgical procedures, diagnostic services, visit types, specialist appointments, and more.

With a privatized system, veterans would be subject to fluctuating payments based on many different criteria. In a private system, different doctors and hospitals have varying rates for the same procedures and services. Also, doctors are paid based on the type of service they perform. As a result, more complicated medical procedures have the capability to quickly increase operating costs.

2. Loss Of Specialized Care

With the current veteran health care system, doctors are frequently exposed to a variety of common ailments that our service members fall victim to.

This includes things like PTSD, amputations, anxiety, and the risk of suicide, rare infectious diseases, and more.

The large volumes of patients that come in with these types of ailments provide the VA doctors with the experience they need to successfully treat patients. If care is shifted to the private sector, it is highly unlikely that a doctor that has the exposure needed to successfully treat these ailments will care for patients.

3. Pricing Fluctuations

Another negative consequence of the privatization of veteran health care is the possibility of pricing fluctuations. With the current system, all facilities and employee salaries are budgeted each year. The cost for medical procedures is paid for at rates that are agreed upon in advance.

However, if the system were to be privatized, those preset spending limits would be gone. The prices for medical care would fluctuate based on the practitioner, the facility, diagnostic tests, and the types of procedures that were being performed. This would result in difficulties planning yearly budgets for veteran health care.

Unfortunately, the decision regarding the privatization of veteran health care is not as clear-cut as many would make it seem. The current system is full of problems like long wait times, limited hospital choices, lack of alternative options, and more. These problems have not been adequately addressed with current legislation.

The closest the government has come to addressing the pitfalls of the current system is the Choice program. This program is designed to provide veterans with alternative care options. However, enrollment involves several stipulations that make it difficult for many veterans to take advantage of the program like a 30-day appointment window and more.

When it comes to the privatization of veteran health care, there are many unknowns that can possibly complicate the problem further. For one, many experts agree that privatization will likely result in higher treatment costs for veterans. Also, a privatized system would result in expenses that are much more difficult to predict.

Due to the many different factors that are involved with this decision, more research and continued debate are required. Only then can we come to a sound decision regarding the privatization of veteran he

The closest the government has come to addressing the pitfalls of the current system is the Choice program. This program is designed to provide veterans with alternative care options. However, enrollment involves several stipulations that make it difficult <u>for many veterans to take advantage of the program</u> like a 30-day appointment window and more.

When it comes to the privatization of veteran health care, there are many unknowns that can possibly complicate the problem further. For one, many experts agree that privatization will likely result in higher treatment costs for veterans. Also, a privatized system would result in expenses that are much more difficult to predict.

Due to the many different factors that are involved with this decision, more research and continued debate are required. Only then can we come to a sound decision regarding the privatization of veteran health care.

23

WIKILEAKS

———

The ""website" WikiLeaks — which would like to be viewed as a news organization has caused a heated debate about the release of diplomatic documents belonging to the United States Government. One of their releases involved confidential information about the Afghanistan war and it is apparent that those leaks cause damage to the U.S. war effort

In a later round of Department of State cables we found out a lot about the gossip and assessment by U.S. diplomats about world leaders and policies. This was certainly embarrassing to the United States.

Is Wikileaks good or bad?

As with all-important things there is a good side and a bad side. It's a double-edged sword at best.

When governments operate in complete secrecy, they often make poor judgments and, in some cases, catastrophic decisions. Transparency is supposed to be the characteristic of democracies. Accountability is the most important benefit of democratic governments where the voters, the people, can kick out governments and bring in better leaders — or arrest and prosecute corrupt or criminal leaders if necessary. In that sense WikiLeaks is good, considering the information they provide is legitimate, and providing lots of information and putting leaders around the world — not just in the U.S. — on notice makes democracy work better.

However, in the conduct of diplomacy and war, confidentiality is often vitally important because diplomacy is a lot like making sausages — it is not something you really want to see because it is messy and smelly.

Should WikiLeaks causes death or destroys the lives of people who are engaged in espionage, war or diplomacy and compromises security and aids rogue governments or terrorists, then that would clearly be bad.

In a later round of releases, if WikiLeaks reveals information about the workings of the banking industry and those revelations show fraud, abuse and criminal conduct, then WikiLeaks is doing the job that the government regulators and prosecutors should be doing, and that would be good and could bring about much-needed reforms of the banking system.

On the other hand if a lot of personal and confidential information is revealed, it could cause identity theft and terrible consequences for individuals, and it could cause a meltdown of some banks and destabilize an already-fragile world financial system — that would be bad.

Should Wikileaks be called a terrorist organization or "traitors"? Well, CNN and the New York Times also often do investigative reporting, get tips and leaks from people and publish information that politicians and leaders want kept secret. Are they terrorist organizations? Are they traitors?

In other parts of the world governments shut down (and worse) newspapers, radio and TV stations, calling them enemies of the people or terrorist. You do not have to look far to find no investigative reporting and no leaks of any kind because the media have been pretty much shut down. Look at what happens in other countries when newspapers or TV report on drug cartels and drug bosses. They are kidnapped, tortured and killed, or the newspaper building is simply blown up with a car bomb.

Governments, politicians, corporations or drug lords have a lot to hide. The difficult issue here is what is legitimate confidentiality and what the public should have the right to know. Until recently the U.S. government stamped "Top Secret" on even the most mundane documents to keep them from the media. Over the past years we pried open some of that, especially with the Freedom of Information Act. Recently the stamp of secrecy has grown in the name of the war on terrorism and the wars in Iraq and Afghanistan.

Remember when the Abu Ghraib prison scandal in Iraq broke and the pictures of Iraqis being humiliated and interrogated made the news.? There was outrage on some quarters that this would undermine the U.S. forces and war effort in Iraq. Yet stopping those types of abuses in the long run quickly deemed by the U.S. military itself as essential to winning the war and the hearts and minds of the people of Iraq. Showing photographs of American war casualties returning in flag-draped coffins was prohibited by the Bush administration. Was that a necessary secrecy?

At what point WikiLeaks oversteps the bounds of reasonable media rights to inform and violate necessary secrecy is a judgment we must make individually in a free society.

24

XENOPHOBIA

—

Xenophobia. It is important to first define the term:" fear and hatred of strangers or foreigners or of anything that is strange or foreign."

A recap of the history of xenophobia in our country is also important to review. The account here is not exhaustive:

When the Europeans began to colonize the Americas, they were faced with a major problem: an indigenous people already populated The Americas. . They dealt with this problem by enslaving and ultimately eliminating most of the indigenous population — reducing it by approximately 95% — and deporting the survivors to undeveloped ghettos that the government, without irony, referred to as "reservations."

These policies could not have been justified if the Native Americans_were treated like human beings. Colonists wrote that American Indians had no religions and no governments, that they practiced "savage" and sometimes physically impossible acts — that they, in short, acceptable victims of genocide. In the United States, this legacy of violent conquest remains largely forgotten.

These actions continued:

1. African Americans

Before 1965, the United States' few non-white immigrants often had to overcome considerable hurdles to settle here. But until 1808 (legally) and for years thereafter (illegally), the United States forcibly recruited African-American immigrants — in chains — to serve as unpaid laborers.

You'd think that a country that had put so much brutal effort into bringing immigrant forced laborers here would at least welcome them when they'd arrived, but the popular view of Africans was that they were violent, amoral savages who could be made useful only if forced to conform to Christian and European traditions. Post-slavery African immigrants have been subjected to many of the same prejudices, and face many of the same stereotypes that existed two centuries ago.

2. English and Scottish Americans

Surely Anglos and Scots have never been subject to xenophobia? After all, the United States was originally an Anglo-American institution, wasn't it?

Well, perhaps not. In the years leading up to the American Revolution, Britain began to be perceived as a villainous empire — and first-generation English immigrants were often viewed with hostility or suspicion. An anti-English sentiment was a significant factor in John Adams' defeat in the 1800 presidential election against the anti-English, pro-French candidate Thomas Jefferson. U.S. opposition to England and Scotland continued up to and including the American Civil War; it was only with the two world wars of the twentieth century that Anglo-U.S. relations finally improved.

3. Chinese Americans

Chinese-American workers began to arrive in large numbers in the late 1840s and helped build many of the railroads that would form the backbone of the emerging U.S. economy. But by 1880 there were some 110,000 Chinese Americans in the country, and some white Americans didn't like the growing ethnic diversity.

Congress responded with the Chinese Exclusion Act of 1882, which stated that Chinese immigration "endangers the good order of certain localities" and would no longer be tolerated. Other responses ranged from bizarre local laws (such as California's tax on the hiring of Chinese-American laborers) to outright violence (such as Oregon's Chinese Massacre of 1887, in which 31 Chinese Americans were murdered by an angry white mob).

4. German Americans

German Americans make up the largest identified ethnic group in the United States today but have historically been subjected to xenophobia as well — primarily during the two World Wars, as Germany and the United States were enemies in both.

During the first World War, or " The Great War" some states went so far as to make it illegal to speak German — a law that was actually enforced on a widespread basis in Montana, and that had a chilling effect on first-generation German-American immigrants living elsewhere.

This anti-German sentiment bubbled up again during the Second World War when some 11,000 German Americans were detained indefinitely by executive order without trials or normal due process protections.

5. Indian Americans

Thousands of Indian Americans had become citizens when the U.S. Supreme Court handed down its ruling in *United States v. Bhagat Singh Thind* (1923), holding that Indians are not white and therefore may not become U.S. citizens by immigration. Thind, an officer for U.S. Army during World War I, initially had his citizenship revoked but was able to quietly immigrate later. Other Indian-Americans were not so lucky and lost both their citizenship and their land.

6. Italian Americans

In October 1890, New Orleans police chief David Hennessy lay dying from bullet wounds he received on his way home from work. Locals blamed Italian-American immigrants, arguing that the "mafia" was responsible for the murder. Police duly arrested 19 immigrants, but had no real evidence against them; charges were dropped against ten of them, and the other nine were acquitted in March of 1891. The day after the acquittal, 11 of the accused were attacked by a white mob and murdered in the streets. Mafia stereotypes affect Italian Americans to this day.

Italy's status as an enemy in World War II was also problematic — leading to arrests, internments, and travel restrictions leveled against thousands of law-abiding Italian-Americans.

7. Japanese Americans

No community was more significantly affected by the World War II "enemy alien" detentions than Japanese Americans. An estimated 110,000 were detained in internment camps during the war, detentions that the U.S. Supreme Court dubiously upheld in *Hirabayashi v. the United States* (1943) and *Korematsu v. the United States* (1944). George Takei, the actor that portrayed Mr. Sulu in Star Trek grew up in a Japanese relocation center in the Western United States when he was a little boy.

Prior to World War II, Japanese-American immigration was most common in Hawaii and California. In California, in particular, some whites resented the presence of Japanese-American farmers and other land-owners — leading to the passage of the California Alien Land Law of 1913, which prohibited Japanese Americans from owning land.

So you see, Xenophobia is nothing new in this country. Pros and Cons? It seems like all Cons, doesn't it? But debate it we will. Every generation.

25

YOGA

—

Yoga and its importance have a bit of controversy associated with it. The Prime Minister of India spoke to the United Nations about the values of yoga. Exercise? Religion? Relaxation technique? The answer is in the eye (or peaceful mind) of the beholder.

What is Yoga?

Yoga is quickly becoming one of the more popular, workout activities among those who are looking to gain flexibility, strength and even lose weight. It can be done from the privacy of your home or at a yoga studio. Yoga is great for reducing stress and allowing for greater relaxation. Once you get into Yoga though, you learn that it is so much more than just a way to workout and keep in shape. It is a philosophy, a passion and a way of life for many of those involved in Yoga. You can choose how much it means to you. While you may be getting into yoga for the exercise, you may soon find yourself wrapped in the philosophy and spirituality that Yoga brings a long with it.

Where Did Yoga Come From?

Yoga is said to have originated in India during the Golden Age, nearly 26,000 years ago. The actual Sanskrit word, when broken down, means "to control", "to yoke" or "to unite". The word has also been translated to mean "joining", "uniting" and "union". The union is made between the self and the spirit. Yoga is a major part of the Hindu religion as it embodies their natural state of being and spiritual enlightenment. As a part of Hinduism, Yoga belongs to one of the six Hindu schools of philosophy. If you dig deeper, you can read about how yoga is used in conjunction with meditation. Yoga is also a major part of Buddhism as a part of their meditation practices. It has even been linked to Islam and early Christianity. So it does have some religious aspects for some adherents.

Yoga today has become increasingly popular, not so much for the spiritual benefits as for the physical advantages. You can take a yoga class at your local gym, a yoga studio or from the privacy of your own home through a personal instructor or a yoga video._From popular musicians embracing Yoga to magazines filled with yoga ads, you simply cannot get away from Yoga and the influence it has had physically and mentally for a lot of folks.

The Benefits of Yoga

Yoga can do a lot for the human body, although it won't cure every ailment. Yoga can be worked into virtually any lifestyle or schedule. Yoga has been proven to increase health and body awareness allowing yoga participants to better control their bodies. From flexibility increases to better body alignment, Yoga can help with a variety of ailments. Many professional athletes practice yoga.

The Physical Benefits of Yoga

- Increased Flexibility
- Increased Strength
- Improved Balance
- Increased Stamina
- Improved Body Alignment (reduces joint pain)

The Mental Benefits of Yoga

- Stress Reduction
- Body Awareness
- Better Sleep
- Improve self-confidence
- Relaxation

There are many more physical and mental benefits, but the major ones are listed above. Those who suffer from certain conditions can also benefit from yoga. Women who are pregnant or who are planning on becoming pregnant can benefit from yoga.

Pros:

1. Yoga is a great stress reliever and helps reduce anxiety.

2. Yoga is a great workout. Even if you aren't engaging in "hot yoga" and sweating your brains out, yoga is still a fantastic way to exercise and lose weight. You improve your flexibility, stamina, and strength and tone your muscles.

3. Yoga improves your brainpower. Yoga and meditation are great for your mind. It improves your memory, helps you to focus, to be present in the moment, challenges your inner strength and increases the blood flow and think more clearly.

4. Yoga is a great detox for your body. Yoga an exercise that massages your internal organs and helps rid the toxins out of your body.

Cons:

1. Price of joining a yoga studio. Yoga can be expensive.

2. That newbie feeling. Starting yoga from scratch in a class full of people who know what they're doing can be a little intimidating.

3. It can be hard to find the right fit. Now there are countless yoga studios and classes in most areas. There are countless teachers in those studios. Not every class or teacher will be the right fit for you. It can be discouraging to take classes and find that you don't enjoy their specific type of teaching.

4. It can be hard to add something else into your busy schedule.

Yoga can be beneficial emotionally, spiritually, and physically. What you get from it is determined not only by what you put into it but what you expect out of it.

The best thing ever? The debate rages on, and perhaps always will.

26

ZOOS

———

Zoos are very controversial. Are they inhumane? Are they in the best interest of the animals? Many zoos are freeing some of the more intelligent species, such as elephants. Aquariams are no longer keeping whales. There is certainly a debate over the necessity, humaneness, and benefits of zoos.

Lets look at some of the pros and cons from a mostly human perspective:

Pros of Zoos:

1. Zoos provide things for animals they would not get in the wild. Excellent nutrition and medical care are but two examples. Not to mention dedicated keepers that have the best interest of the animals at heart

2.Reearch and educational opportunities.
Zoos allow children and adults to observe wild animals, an opportunity that is normally not possible for many people. Having exotic and large animals secured in enclosures, these places also allow researchers and scientists to perform scientific studies to better help us understand these animals. This could be of benefit in saving more of them.

3. Zoos help some animals survive..
Out in the wild, some animals would have a very little chance to survive, especially those on the endangered species list. Many animals are still hunted by poachers for their skins, bones and other by-products. Also, some of them have a more difficult time surviving in the wild by themselves due to pollution, destruction of their habitats, high level of competition for food, over-predation, diseases and other reasons.

4. Zoos utilize good conservation programs under strict and beneficial regulations.
Captive breeding programs are implemented to help preserve animals that have decreased in number, which is a good way to prevent the extinction of some species. Also, the government and involved organizations normally set strict regulations for zoos to follow, which require regular check-ups on resident animals and rigid procedures to acquire new ones.

5. Safety and security for animals, which they may not otherwise have in the wild, are provided.

Cons of Zoos:

1. Zoos pose several risks that particularly affect animals.
There are many problems that come with keeping animals in zoos. One of them is the confined spaces where the animals are forced to live in. Unlike their natural habitats where they can freely roam, these establishments keep them confined.

This is even worse for animals that need to migrate and move around a lot. For example, elephants normally travel long distances in groups, and by confining them into smaller spaces, it definitely goes against their migratory nature. Aside from elephants, other animals, such as lions, will not get the chance to hunt, making them more aggressive if they are not properly taken care of. This can arise more danger for zoo personnel, as well as visitors. Zoo animals are basically prisoners. They are without freedom.

2. Natural animal behaviors are changed in captivity.
Captured animals that are brought to the zoos tend to develop behavioral problems, which causes concern for the overall well-being of all the resident animals, and the human keepers.

3. Zoos have a negative impact on the mental conditions of animals.

For those captured from the wild, it takes a long time for them to adjust to being confined, and once they manage to adjust, they will be very stressed from the adjustment experience. And for animals that are born in the zoo, it would be like a double-edged sword for them because being released to the wild risks their survival, as they do not have the natural capabilities to hunt and cope for themselves.

4. Zoos are seen as places for human amusement.

Though zoos are seen positively when it comes to the aspect of entertainment, the fact that animals are captured and placed in captivity for the sole purpose of human amusement is one of the main reasons of the existing anti-zoo campaigns.

5. Many of the zoo establishments are struggling financially.

There are high costs associated with maintaining the resident animals against the lesser income from the visits by park customers and other funds. When this happens, a zoo would usually close down, leading to the animals either getting divided to be accommodated to other zoos, animal rescues or animals getting sold off to cover the debts the affected zoo might have incurred. What's worse, the animals do not always go to people who may have their best interests in mind. For these reason, zoos can be detrimental for not just the animals in them, but for the staff as well.

6. Conservation is sometimes a pointless gesture.

While these establishments are really trying to do their best to let animals mate, their offspring are normally kept at the same zoo or simply moved to another one, which does nothing for the numbers of the species in the wild.

Zoos provide both good outcomes and bad outcomes for the animals they keep. Though they provide a lot of benefits for researchers, they do come at a cost, whether it is worth the risk or not. For many people, zoos represent an opportunity to experience seeing species that would be impossible to see otherwise. It all boils down to zoos serving a function as an educational, entertainment and research solution, in addition to providing animals a place to be secure. Is it fair for the animals in house? By weighing the pros and cons, you will be able to come up with a well-informed decision. The debate will continue.

Here is a list of the five largest Zoos in the world:

1. Berlin Zoological Garden.
2. The Columbus Zoo and Aquarium.
3. The Toronto Zoo.
4. The Beijing Zoo.
5. The Henry Doorly Zoo and Aquarium.

DEBATES WE WILL BE HAVING THIS CENTURY

1. Terrorism
2. Death Penalty
3. Climate Change.
4. Stem Cell Research.
5. Privacy.
6. Technologies impact on jobs.
7. Global Trade.
8. Income inequality.
9. Competent Government.
10. Reproductive Rights.
11. Education.
12. Agriculture.
13. Energy Policy.
14. The War on Drugs.
15. Money in politics/Gerrymandering/ the Electoral College.
16. Policing.
17. Clean Water.
18. Food Availability.
19. Corporate Regulation.
20. Struggles of the Free Press.

www.ingramcontent.com/pod-product-compliance
Lightning Source LLC
Chambersburg PA
CBHW050909260726
48660CB00001B/117